PROTECTING CHILDREN AND YOUNG PEOPLE

Children and Organised Sport

PROTECTING CHILDREN AND YOUNG PEOPLE

SERIES EDITORS

ANNE STAFFORD and **SHARON VINCENT**
The University of Edinburgh / NSPCC Centre
for UK-wide Learning in Child Protection

CHILDREN AND ORGANISED SPORT

Kate Alexander and Anne Stafford

Published by
Dunedin Academic Press Ltd
Hudson House
8 Albany Street
Edinburgh EH1 3QB
Scotland

ISBN: 978–1-906716–24–0
ISSN: 1756–0691

First Published 2011
© Kate Alexander and Anne Stafford

British Library Cataloguing in Publication data
A catalogue record for this book is available from the British Library

Typeset by Makar Publishing Production, Edinburgh
Printed and bound in Great Britain by CPI Antony Rowe,
Chippenham and Eastbourne

Contents

Acknowledgements

The authors would like to acknowledge the support of those who contributed in various ways to the research upon which this book is based, in particular to Ruth Lewis, Naomi Marks, Michelle Opit and Amanda Thomson. The support of our colleagues in the Centre for Learning in Child Protection was also invaluable: they commented on drafts, helped shape our research and made time for discussion which helped clarify our thinking at many points along the way. We want to thank the NSPCC for funding the work and to express gratitude to individual members of NSPCC staff: Phillip Noyes and staff in the Child Protection Sport Unit (CPSU) in particular, for supporting the work through some early hiccups and for providing ongoing advice and support. Not least, we want to thank the young people themselves who took the time to complete our lengthy and sometimes difficult questionnaire, and who took part in our interviews.

Glossary

In conducting our research, we did not define our language except in cases where the words might be unfamiliar. Therefore, research participants' own understanding of terms such as 'once or twice', 'regularly', or 'most of your childhood', determined the answers they gave. However, there are a few terms used throughout the text that require explanation.

MAIN AND SECOND SPORT
Respondents were asked to give their main sport from a predefined list. They were subsequently asked if they participated in more than one sport and, if they did, were asked to give the sport they considered to be their second sport. They were given guidance to choose the sports they 'would consider to be the most influential in your life, either positively or negatively'.

ORGANISED SPORT
Organised sport was defined in the study as sport that is voluntary, takes place outside school hours and includes an element of training or instruction by an adult. Respondents to the survey were given this definition in the questionnaire. They were given further guidance not to include PE lessons and informally arranged sport such as 'kick-abouts' with friends. They were asked to include extra-curricular sport at school: for example, playing in the school team or being part of a club, based at school but taking place outside ordinary PE lessons.

TOP SEVEN SPORTS
When considering young people's experience of sport in the following chapters, some analysis will be presented by main and second sport and in most instances this will be limited to the top seven sports reported in the survey. This includes all sports reported by

more than 10% of respondents (swimming, netball, football, dance, hockey and athletics). To these we have added rugby which, although reported by just 8% of participants as a whole, was played by a quarter of boys as either their main or second sport. This made it the second most popular sport among boys, after football.

TYPES OF HARM

In our research, we defined emotional harm, sexual harassment, sexual harm and physical harm through sets of behaviours, shown below. In reporting our results, respondents experiencing any of these types of harm are those who said they had experienced at least one of these behaviours either 'once or twice' or 'regularly', in either their main or second sport. Within the text, we also make reference to definitions of these types of harm from the literature.

Emotional harm

The set of behaviours defining emotional harm are:
- being embarrassed or humiliated;
- being bullied about something;
- being teased about something;
- being criticised about your looks/weight;
- being criticised about your performance;
- being shouted or sworn at;
- being called names;
- being ignored in a way that made you feel bad;
- being criticised/threatened for not wanting to train/compete;
- having lies or rumours spread about you;
- having your things damaged/stolen to humiliate/threaten you;
- being threatened with being thrown out of the club;
- being threatened with being hit but not actually being hit.

Sexual harassment

The set of behaviours defining sexual harassment are:
- being subject to sexist jokes;
- being whistled or leered at;
- having sexual comments made about your appearance, etc.;
- having your space invaded;
- physical contact that made you uncomfortable;

- being touched in instruction in a way that made you uncomfortable;
- having a massage or rub that made you uncomfortable;
- excessive phone calls at home that made you uncomfortable;
- being sent letters/cards/emails/texts with a sexual content;
- invitations to be alone with someone;
- excessive compliments or criticism about your appearance;
- excessive compliments or criticism about your performance;
- inconsistent treatment (sometimes singled out, sometimes ignored).

Sexual harm

The set of behaviours defining sexual harm are:
- being forced to kiss someone;
- having someone expose themselves to you;
- being touched sexually against your will;
- someone trying to have sex with you against your will;
- being forced to have penetrative sex (oral, vaginal or anal).

Physical harm

The set of behaviours defining physical harm are:
- being forced to train when injured/ exhausted;
- being shoved;
- being shaken;
- being thrown about;
- being knocked down;
- having something thrown at you;
- being forcefully restrained;
- being hit with an open hand;
- being hit with a fist;
- being hit with an implement;
- being choked (grabbed around neck);
- being beaten up.

Introduction

RESEARCHING CHILD ABUSE AND MALTREATMENT

The first major study into the extent of maltreatment in the general population took place in 1999 and gathered information from young adults aged eighteen to twenty-four about their childhood experiences, including their experiences of physical, sexual and emotional abuse and neglect (Cawson *et al.*, 2000). This National Society for the Prevention of Cruelty to Children (NSPCC) report was the first and, until the publication of a recently completed new prevalence study, remains the only comprehensive study in the UK of child maltreatment. The prevalence study provided reliable baseline information about the extent and nature of child maltreatment and abuse.

In developing baseline information about the prevalence of types of child maltreatment, the authors of the prevalence study considered the difficulties besetting work of this kind. Definitions of abuse change over time and vary according to culture. Attempting to obtain single figures representing the proportion of the population who have been abused in various ways can mask differences in individual experiences, and this creates difficulties in dealing with overlapping patterns of abuse; and rates of abuse may differ according to whether they are professionally assessed or self-assessed (Cawson *et al.*, 2000).

Against the background of these acknowledged difficulties, the prevalence study (Cawson *et al.*, 2000) found that a quarter of the sample had experienced at least one type of physical abuse. Most physical abuse was perpetrated by parents or carers but 7% was perpetrated by a professional person. Eleven per cent of the sample had experienced sexual abuse by adults known to them but not related to them; this was the largest category of sexual abuse. Four per cent had been abused by parents or other family members, and 4% by strangers. The area of emotional or psychological abuse was acknowledged to be the most difficult to measure. Six per cent of the sample was assessed as having been emotionally maltreated; more than half had experienced at least one of the behaviours explored.

The NSPCC prevalence study (Cawson *et al.*, 2000) did not specifically ask young people about negative experiences in a sport setting. However, since then there has been a growing research and policy interest in the treatment of children and young people in sport, particularly in the light of high-profile abuse cases within specific sports. For example, the prosecution and conviction of Paul Hickson, the former Olympic swimming coach for the rape and sexual abuse of teenagers in his elite squad, triggered the NSPCC study *In at the Deep End* (Myers and Barret, 2002). It found that there was a 'significant minority of children and young people suffering sexual, emotional and verbal abuse at the hands of those in respected and powerful positions within the sport', and that in the case of child sexual abuse there can be a process of grooming by coaches who manipulate the respect they have developed over a period of years. Although similar work has been conducted looking at the experience of children in specific sports, no research has looked at the experience of children across sports and in sport at all levels, from recreational to elite-level competition.

This book emerged from a three-year study funded by NSPCC, which aimed to address this gap in knowledge about harm to children in sport and, in the context of their experiences as a whole, to investigate the range of maltreatment and negative experiences they might face while participating in organised sport. The study combined a literature review with a survey of young people aged eighteen to twenty-two; then in-depth interviews with a subset of survey respondents. The survey, which achieved more than 6,000 returns, explored young people's experiences of different types of harm in organised sport when they were children. The interviews gathered more detailed information about these experiences and explored their feelings about this.

CHILDREN'S RIGHTS

The United Nations Convention on the Rights of the Child (UNCRC) provides a useful framework within and through which to explore how children should be treated in various contexts (including sport) (United Nations, 1989). The Convention sets out the civil, political, economic, social, and cultural rights of children. It is binding on all states that ratify it — currently, this means all members of the United Nations with the exception of the United States and Somalia. It is one of seven human rights treaties that constitute the core of international human rights law, and it came into force in 1990. States that ratify it are subject to international scrutiny through the UN Committee on the Rights of the Child.

The importance of the Convention is that it has moved consideration of the way children are treated in societies across the world from one based on welfare or needs to one based on entitlements (David, 2005). Many of the articles set out in the Convention have resonance for the treatment of children participating in sport. In Article 3, the Convention establishes the principle of 'the best interests of the child', which is expected to guide all actions related to the child by public and private bodies in states ratifying the Convention. The specific rights contained are wide ranging and include basic rights such as the right to life and development (Article 6); the right to an identity and to have that identity recognised and protected by the state (Articles 7 and 8); and the right to health and health care (Articles 24 and 25). Also included are rights to protection against maltreatment and exploitation such as abuse, neglect and violence (Article 19); economic exploitation (Article 32); illegal drugs (Article 33); sexual exploitation and abuse, and trafficking and abduction (Article 35); rights to education (Articles 28 and 29) and to rest, leisure, play and a cultural life (Article 31); rights to family life (Articles 9, 10, 18 and 21); and rights to freedom of expression (Articles 13 and 14), association (Article 15) and to have their views taken into account (Article 12). All of the rights contained in the Convention apply to all children regardless of race, colour, sex, language, religion, political or other opinion, national, ethnic or social origin, property, disability, birth or other status (Article 2). There is also the recognition within the

Convention of the 'evolving capacities of the child' to exercise his or her own rights (Article 5).

The United Kingdom ratified the Convention in 1991, although it registered some reservations. However, the Convention has not been incorporated into UK law, which means that children and young people cannot take a case to court if they believe that their rights under the Convention have been breached. Nevertheless, the Convention should be referred to in court and all other proceedings affecting children and should always inform interpretations and judgements in Human Rights Act cases brought by children.

By 2005, following extensive campaigning by organisations and individuals concerned with children's welfare and children's rights, each of the four jurisdictions in the UK had in place a commissioner for children. Their roles and remits differ slightly, but all have a role in promoting the rights enshrined in the Convention and in ensuring children's views are sought on issues affecting them. An evaluation of the commissioner for Wales in 2008 found that, although awareness of the commissioner's office among children generally was low, effective work had been done to engage with children and to learn from them.

These developments have contributed to a policy and practice environment in which the experience of children in a range of arenas is increasingly examined through the lens of children's rights. While not specifically mentioning sport, Article 31 of the Convention confers rights to leisure and play. The Convention also refers to children's relationships with their states, families and education, all of which may be relevant to their participation in organised sport. Throughout this book, we will return to the framework of children's rights to evaluate the experience of the young people who took part in our research.

STRUCTURE OF THE BOOK

This introduction continues by giving an overview of the participants in our research. In Chapter 1, we discuss the positive and negatives of participating in sport as described by participants in our study. Chapter 2 provides an overview of the types of harm children may face in sport, using existing literature and information from our own study. In Chapter 3, we introduce the notion of the sport ethic — where pain and injury are accepted as 'the norms' in sport. We also describe the process by which young athletes internalise this and adapt to it. We also consider the development of particular sporting cultures at different levels of competition and in different sports. Chapter 4 looks at the role of coaches and other adults as perpetrators of harm, both through coaching practice and by their complicity in harm by peers. Chapter 5 considers the role of team mates and peers as the perpetrators of harm in sport. It also looks at the extent to which children tend to accept maltreatment as normal and are reluctant to see it as harmful; rather they view it as a necessary part of sporting participation, toughening up and growing up. Finally, in Chapter 6, we consider the ways in which those involved in organised sport can ensure that it is a safe, positive and happy experience for children.

RESEARCH PARTICIPANTS

The questionnaire survey for our research achieved over 6,000 returns from young people throughout the UK who had been asked to describe their experiences of sport as children — 73% from young women and 27% from young men. While men were under-represented, the absolute number of male respondents was high enough to allow meaningful interpretation and comparison of the findings. Ten per cent of respondents gave their ethnicity as something other than white, broadly in line with the proportion for the population as a whole. Ninety-three per cent gave their sexual orientation as straight. Six per cent of respondents considered themselves to have a disability and 1% participated in disabled sport as children.

By far the most common childhood family structure was a two-parent (or guardian) household (87%). Less than 1% had spent most of their childhood in circumstances other than a one- or two-parent family. Similarly, less than 1% of survey respondents had experienced residential care or foster care at any point in their childhood.

The respondents comprised young people from a slightly higher socio-economic group than the population of young people as a whole. Around one-third of parents had an undergraduate degree or higher — a considerably higher proportion than the 21% reported to the Labour Force Survey of 2008 (Hughes, 2009).

Against this background, Chapter 1 looks at sport participation and uses the testimony of research participants to explore the positives and negatives of taking part in organised sport.

Positives and negatives of organised sport

Introduction

Sport is often presented in the mainstream literature as universally positive and sometimes as a solution to societal problems, such as obesity and deprivation. In the run-up to the 2012 Olympic Games in London, there has been a focus on the positive aspects of sport participation and the encouragement of children and young people to lead more active lives through sport. However, recent research is beginning to challenge ideological assumptions that sport is wholly positive and beneficial (Coakley, 2007). Over the past twenty-five years, a growing body of work has begun to probe athletes' negative experiences of sport. This has included increasing awareness of physical harm incurred through sport; the excessive pressure and stress that young athletes may experience, particularly at elite level (Coakley, 1992; David, 2005); and the maltreatment of athletes (Stirling, 2009). Competitive youth sport has also been critiqued from a children's rights perspective (David, 2005; Farstad, 2007).

This chapter begins by giving an overview of youth participation in organised sport both from the literature and from our own research. It then considers the positive and negative aspects of taking part in sport. It raises some of the themes we will return to in later chapters and provides a broader context for the discussion of harm in sport that follows.

YOUTH PARTICIPATION IN ORGANISED SPORT

Sport plays a major part in the lives of many children and young people in the UK. Youth participation in organised sport is correlated with demographic factors, such as age and sex. Participation in extra-curricular physical activity appears to peak around eleven, and then diminish as children reach their teenage years (Sports Council Wales, 2009; Smith *et al.*, 2007). Among primary-aged children, extra-curricular physical activity is evenly balanced between the sexes, but among older children (eleven to sixteen year olds), boys are more likely to participate than girls (Sports Council Wales, 2009). Declining female participation in sport over the teenage years is widely documented (Smith *et al.*, 2007; Coleman *et al.*, 2008; Niven *et al.*, 2009). Early sporting experiences, particularly regarding PE kit, privacy, body image and the dominance of boys appear to influence older girls' lower participation in sport (Foster *et al.*, 2005). Young people with a disability are also less likely than able-bodied children to participate in organised sport, with lack of money, lack of suitable facilities and transport difficulties commonly cited by young people as barriers to greater participation (Finch, 2001). Furthermore, there has been growing acknowledgement by the UK sports councils that homophobia and related discrimination are likely to influence lesbian, gay, bisexual and transgender (LGBT) participation in organised sport, although specific data on LGBT youth participation in sport is scarce (Brackenridge, 2008).

The most popular activities for eight to fifteen year olds in Scotland in 2005–2007 were football, swimming, cycling, dance and running/jogging (sportscotland, 2008). However, these popular sporting activities do not always involve participation through a club. In terms of organised sport, judo and martial arts are the activities children in Scotland are most likely to undertake as members of a club; followed by shinty, dance and gymnastics (ibid.). Sports with the biggest club memberships among young people in England in 2002 were football, swimming, and martial arts (Sport England, 2003b). In Wales, 78% of primary-aged children (one to eleven year olds) and 73% of secondary-aged children (eleven to sixteen year olds) participated in club-based sport in 2004 (Sport Council Wales, 2006).

The definition of 'organised sport' used in our research was slightly broader than club sports, because we included extra-curricular sport at school. The majority of young people who responded to the survey competed above recreational level. Thirteen per cent of respondents to the survey competed nationally or internationally in their main sport. Young women were more likely to say their main sport remained recreational (30% compared to 21% of young men) but, apart from this, gender differences were minimal, with equal proportions of young men and women competing at elite level.

Respondents participated in more than forty organised sports as either their main sport or second sport. A wide range of both individual and team sports were represented but just six sports were played by more than 10% of respondents (swimming, netball, football, dance, hockey and athletics). Unsurprisingly, there were gender differences: for example, netball and dance were almost exclusively reported by girls, while football and rugby were predominantly played by boys. Of the top ten sports in the survey just athletics, tennis and badminton had similar proportions of boys and girls reporting participation.

POSITIVE ASPECTS OF SPORT IN GENERAL

Sport for children has been encouraged on the assumption that it promotes the citizenship, autonomy and welfare of young people (Brackenridge, 2002). In addition to the physical health benefits that come from active lives, studies have suggested that sport can offer some protection from mental ill health, such as depression, in young people. It has also been linked to increased confidence and enhanced self-esteem (Sport England, 2003b). Furthermore, childhood participation in sport and physical activity makes adult participation much more likely than non-participation (ibid.).

Much of the existing research concerning children's experiences of sport has focused on elite child athletes competing on the national and international stage. However, as most young people participate at lower levels, such as school, local or district clubs, it is important to understand children's experiences across different levels of participation in a range of sports. Eighty-seven per cent of participants in our research took part in their main sport at levels below national level. In second sport this proportion rose to 95%. Addressing one gap in research knowledge, these views tell us more about competition at lower levels than at elite level.

Young people who took part were asked to discuss the positives and negatives of participating in sport; also whether positives outweighed negatives, or vice versa. Many themes from the literature were echoed in their answers.

When asked to describe the atmosphere in their sports clubs, by far the most common words used by survey respondents were 'fun' and 'competitive'. Words closely connected to 'fun' were also in the top twenty words used: 'enjoyable', 'friendly', 'co-operative' and 'exciting'. Where these aspects of club life were encouraged and promoted, fun and competitiveness were a positive combination:

> The basketball team was a lot of fun. We had a really cool coach. He was just, he was one of the guys who just worked in the department. He took us on. So that was always a lot of fun. It was definitely like competitive. But it was always competitive against the other team. So, I would have thought that would be a very positive competitiveness. Like, you know, it wasn't like competing against ourselves or, you didn't have to be the best or anything like that. It was just, you know, when you get on the pitch, you know, you do your best, all that stuff. But it was never like a crazy drive. So the basketball team it was great. That was a lot of fun. (*Young man: main sport football; second sport basketball*)

Figure 1.1 provides a visual representation of young people's answers to the question in the survey about the best thing about organised sport as a child. It clearly shows that here too the social aspects were most likely to be mentioned — meeting new people, friends and fun being frequently given as answers. Young people also talked about learning skills, keeping fit and being active.

When asked to expand on these themes at interview, young people talked of developing life-long friends through sport, often with people who came from different backgrounds:

> I think mainly just meeting loads of people. Like you get to see like different people you don't know, get to meet different cultures and stuff. And you just come across totally different people that you wouldn't normally hang around with. (*Young woman: main sport rugby; second sport hockey*)

Some young people spoke of how the process of meeting different people through sport built their confidence and enabled them to feel comfortable in a range of different situations, unrelated to sport.

Figure 1.1: 'Wordle' of the 50 most common words when young people were asked to give the best thing about being involved in organised sport

Learning a new skill, being good at something and having a sense of achievement were also positive. These could also be linked to developing a sense of self-confidence and self-esteem — attributes young people considered to be useful in later life:

> I think for me the biggest positives were always the feeling of achievement. And the, the actual, the sort of boost to my confidence when I got something right and when I was praised for it ... I was always pushing myself to be the best I could. And when, when I did something absolutely perfectly and it was recognised that was just the ultimate kind of gratification I suppose. And ... yeah so that, I mean it did, I think it did build my confidence a lot, certainly initially. (*Young woman: main sport gymnastics; second sport equestrian sports*)

Being part of a team, learning to work together with a group of people regardless of whether they were friends, was also seen as an important positive element of being involved in organised sport. Young people recognised that a team needed a range of skills, personalities and talents to make it effective and that people who were not the 'starriest' players had important roles within teams:

> I think the experiences you have as part of a team are irreplaceable. I mean you don't necessarily have to be best of friends with people that you play in a team with, but you kind of bond anyway, regardless if these are children that

you would have been friends with in the playground as it were. It definitely gave me a huge amount of self-esteem. I was quite a chubby little kid in primary school, and I think hockey was the first thing I started playing, and, you know, just the confidence of realising that it doesn't matter if you are fat you can still play sport and you can still be good at it was hugely beneficial. I think as well self-esteem, confidence, definitely. I was never the best at anything by any means. I was never of a very good standard. But, you know, I was enthusiastic and people appreciated that I think. (*Young woman: main sport hockey; second sport football*)

Keeping fit and active were other positive aspects of being involved in organised sport, and some mentioned it as a means of counteracting the more sedentary lives of young people today:

Yeah and I mean with the sports as well it also helps kind of, with kids especially nowadays with all the computers and all that it's kind of hard to encourage them to go outside. So I think it was like really important to encourage us to do something physical as well. (*Young woman: main sport equestrian sports; second sport fencing*)

The views expressed by research participants about the positive aspects of sport mirror the benefits that are ascribed to sporting participation in the literature and in programmes to promote youth sport. Young participants valued the opportunities sport gave them to improve their health, skills and social lives.

GENERAL NEGATIVE ASPECTS OF SPORT PARTICIPATION

A growing body of research highlights some of the more negative impacts of sport. However, as the next chapter will show, much of the research conducted to date has tended to focus on the experiences of adult athletes, often at elite level. Where the focus is on children, most research activity has also considered the experience of those athletes who reached high levels of attainment in their sport, or has considered the issues experienced by children and young people competing in a particular sport such as football or swimming. However, a national survey of young people's participation in sport in

England in 2002 found that among the negative aspects of sport for young people were 'going outside in bad weather' (42%), 'getting cold and wet' (36%) and 'getting hot and sweaty' when playing sport (36%) (Sport England, 2003b). Among primary and secondary school pupils in Wales, the most commonly cited barrier to extracurricular participation in sport was a lack of time (Sports Council Wales, 2009). Our research considered the experiences of children competing at all levels, and across a range of sports. The negative aspects highlighted by young people reflect this broad scope.

In common with the Welsh study quoted above, the time commitment involved in participating in organised sport was the biggest negative cited by research participants. Young people sometimes felt torn between the demands of their sport and their desire to involve themselves fully in the social and educational opportunities that were also available:

> Yeah, and the training was hard, and school, like the stuff, well I was taking a lot of subjects, and I felt I was missing out on a bit of like the social stuff, but at the same time I knew it was my choice, and there wasn't that much time left at school so I just knew that I would go through with it, and also because I didn't feel like I could turn round and say to my coaches sorry I know you have put loads of time and effort into making me better, but I just don't want to do it any more, didn't … I felt that would be kind of horrible to them because they showed me a lot of kindness and stuff, by taking me into the squad. (*Young woman: main sport gymnastics; second sport hockey*)

Young people also found that the atmosphere of their sport could be overly competitive, particularly as they advanced through the competitive ranks. This was reflected in the fact that among the top twenty words used to describe the atmosphere in sports clubs were words that might be associated with 'competitive' in a more negative way such as 'aggressive' and 'hard'. Young people felt that while competing as children they were in a position where they would let down the whole team and their coach if they were perceived not to be playing at their best. The prospect of failure was ever present:

> If you are competing you've got the potential to fail on like a weekly basis, especially with things like swimming, the training is very intense for someone if they want to carry on for like their GCSEs and that kind of thing. It does pretty much take over your life. (*Young woman: main sport canoeing/kayaking; second sport swimming*)

This intensely competitive atmosphere could become a source of pressure for young people: pressure to take part, pressure to drop other commitments, pressure to play well and pressure to win. Again, young people linked an increase in this pressure to higher levels of competition, and noted that pressure could come from a variety of sources:

> Yeah. Well, I mean you didn't really have much choice in things. If there was a match going on at the weekend that you had like another commitment you had to go to, and I don't think it was really understood that you'd rather go to this other thing than a match. Like yeah, I think there was a lot of pressure from the teachers but a lot of pressure from like team mates if, like, especially when I left, when, yeah, cause they had to replace you, and there was a limited number of people in our school who were willing or wanted to play sport. Obviously that was tricky, yeah. This was I think only when I was pushing myself a bit too hard. Like in the early days there was a lot less pressure. (*Young woman: main sport hockey; second sport football*)

Young people also reported a range of negative experiences of emotional harm, bullying, physical harm, sexualised behaviour and sexual harm associated with sport, and these will be considered in greater detail in the chapters that follow. However, when asked to comment more generally on the negative aspects of sport, the issues that predominated were those of balancing their sporting activities with other parts of their social lives and the way in which becoming more skilled at their sports could sometimes bring with it increased pressure.

THE ROLE OF ADULTS

Prior literature highlights the important role adults play in the sporting lives of children. They are present in a range of roles such as coach, club official, volunteer helper and parent supporter. In our study too, the adults involved exerted a significant influence on the sporting experience of young people. In many cases, this influence was positive. Young people spoke warmly about the encouragement and support they received from adults involved in their sports, particularly coaches:

> Yeah, I couldn't say anything bad about any of the coaches I've had, or any of the people that were involved. They were never too hard on us, and always encouraging, and we were rewarded and we did have a laugh with them as well. I don't think I can say anything bad about them. (*Young woman: main sport netball; second sport gymnastics*)

In some circumstances, coaches provided role models for the children they coached, in terms of sporting achievements, commitment to a sport and a club, and enjoyment of the social aspects of being involved in a sport. One young woman described how her coach and other adults set the tone of her fencing club and worked hard to make it a place of learning and encouragement:

> Oh yeah definitely. In fencing we were actually very lucky because our coach was a very, he had like won awards and stuff like that. So he was very high level and he was also brilliantly friendly, very encouraging. It was really thanks to him that a lot of people stayed in the clubs. There was other adults as well but, that played a big part ... A lot of people were there, had been there throughout the years. They joined when they were quite young and then they stayed on. And yeah they all played, they took the young ones and like taught them the basics. And then Andy the main coach, he kind of concentrated more on the older ones. But you got a lot of encouragement. And it, they encouraged it to be friendly and everything else. (*Young woman: main sport equestrian sports; second sport fencing*)

There were also examples of adults actively fostering team building and the positive aspects of team work through trips away and events — that is, through activities other than training and competing:

> I can remember going off to some camp thing somewhere, like the kind of cliché team-building exercise, things like that. I can never remember looking back like any kind of hostile situations between people either. Everything was always quite calm atmosphere, you know. I am guessing they created that or facilitated it at least. (*Young man: main sport rugby; second sport athletics*)

The adults could also exert a negative influence on young people's sporting experience. Some young people mentioned that parents' behaviour could be upsetting both for their own children and for other young athletes:

> There were a few parents, I can remember one in particular who wasn't always that pleasant, sort of shouting from side-lines, and I remember feeling quite sorry for her daughter because they was always very hard on her. (*Young woman: main sport netball; second sport gymnastics*)

Sometimes, adults could have split loyalties, particularly at recreational level where there was a heavy reliance on volunteers who were parents of team members. This could be experienced as negative and demotivating by other players:

> Yeah, well like there's … I tended to find that there was quite a big difference, certainly down our way and in Devon, the corner country like, it's probably the same like most areas, that age group that it's generally just volunteers or people's parents, so obviously they're looking out for their kid at the same time. Some I found did kind of help with that, and others that didn't particularly feel like they were there for helping the whole team if you know what I mean. Yeah, like a couple of people you were just kind of like they are looking out for their son and that's it. It gets a bit annoying when it's like that. (*Young man: main sport rugby; second sport football*)

In Chapter 5 we will consider further the negative role adults, particularly coaches, can play in relation to children's sporting experience.

CONCLUSION

This chapter has given an overview of young people's positive and negative experiences of sport. Elsewhere in our survey and in the subsequent interviews, we asked specifically about harmful experiences and, as we will demonstrate in the following chapters, a majority had experienced some emotional harm; and large minorities had experienced other forms of harm.

Nevertheless, at interview, when asked if positives outweighed the negatives or vice versa, almost all said that the positives far outweighed the negatives. In addition, all of the young people we interviewed said that they would encourage their own children to become involved in sport. However, as we shall see in Chapter 6, this encouragement was not unconditional. Rather, it was qualified by a concern that some of the negatives they experienced should be addressed; that children should be happy when playing sport and the experience should be enjoyable, and as far as possible stress free.

CHAPTER 2

Child maltreatment in sport

Introduction

In this chapter we discuss the kinds of harm children may face in sport, drawing information from previous studies and from our own research.

Increasing awareness of abuse and harm within sport partly mirrors growing concern about child welfare and child abuse over the past few decades. Gervis and Dunn (2004) have highlighted the importance of the coach–athlete relationship for child elite athletes; some young people can perceive the relationship as more important than that with their parents. Farstad (2007) has also noted how this intensity can provide a fertile ground for the development of abusive coaching relationships:

> The potential for abuse and violence increases in situations where intense rela-
> tionships exist between children or young people and adults who have consider-
> able influence over them. Such relationships often develop in competitive sports
> when sports coaches and their students spend long hours together. Much of their
> time is spent together at conventions and in hotels away from home and away
> from parental control. (Farstad, 2007, p.6)

Previous research on harm in sport has focused on that perpetrated by coaches, even though perpetrators may be other authority figures, including medical staff, administrative staff, janitors or bus drivers (Brackenridge *et al.*, 2006; Myers and Barret, 2002). In addition, there is increasing acknowledge-ment of peers as potential perpetrators of harm within sports settings (David, 2005; Brackenridge *et al.*, 2006). We provide further insights into the role of peers as perpetrators of harm later in this chapter, then go into more detail in Chapter 5. Earlier research has also tended to focus on three main areas of harm — sexual harm, physical harm and emotional harm. The rest of this chapter explores these in the context of our research.

SEXUAL HARM

More research has been carried out on sexual harassment and abuse in sport than other forms of harm such as emotional harm, physical harm and neglect. Nevertheless, research in this area is still relatively recent, with studies beginning in the mid-1980s. These early studies on sexual harm in sport largely focused on female athletes' experiences, emerging from earlier focus on harassment in the workplace and educational settings (Fasting, 2005).

On the other hand, research on childhood sexual abuse has mostly focused on intra-familial abuse; and since the 1980s there has been increasing awareness of the institutional abuse of children, particularly in residential care settings, boarding schools and church organisations (Gallagher, 2000). However, although vast numbers of children participate in organised sport, and despite several high-profile convictions in the 1990s, youth sport has received only relatively limited research attention in relation to sexual harassment and harm.

We noted in the Introduction that there are no universally accepted definitions of various types of harm to children. In the case of sexual harassment and harm, the position is complicated further by the difficulty of drawing a distinction between the two, with some research indicating a 'grey area' between them (Fasting, 2005; Nielsen, 2001). Furthermore, many studies not only use harassment and abuse interchangeably, but also make no reference to the age of the parties involved, so it is difficult to distinguish between child and adult athletes (Bringer et al., 2006, p. 466). Brackenridge (2001) has proposed a sexual exploitation continuum in sport, which outlines different types and degrees of unwanted sexual experiences, making the important point that despite objective definitions of such behaviours they are experienced subjectively. This continuum incorporates sexual discrimination, sexual harassment and sexual abuse (Brackenridge, 2001). She also notes the artificial distinction between sexual abuse and other types of exploitative or abusive practices. Certainly, wider research on child maltreatment indicates that histories of childhood sexual abuse are associated with other forms of abuse and neglect during childhood (Cawson *et al.*, 2000; Dong *et al.*, 2003; Whitfield *et al.*, 2005).

A further issue is young athletes' perception of their experiences and whether they define what happened to them as harm or harassment. In their study of child maltreatment in the UK, Cawson *et al.* (2000) noted that studies have moved away from attempting comprehensive definitions of abuse towards examining the occurrence of a range of behaviours. This is the approach adopted by our own study.

Prevalence of sexual harassment and sexual harm

The prevalence of sexual harassment and sexual harm in sport has been more widely researched than other forms of harm. However, many studies focus on the sexual harassment and abuse of athletes over the age of sixteen. There are few data on the childhood prevalence of sexual harm in sport, and little is known about the extent of sexual harm of children in UK sport.

Quantitative studies investigating the prevalence of sexual harassment and abuse in sport have been conducted in a number of countries including: the USA (Volkwein *et al.*, 1997), Canada (Kirby *et al.*, 2000), Australia (Leahy *et al.*, 2002), Denmark (Nielsen, 2001), Norway (Fasting *et al.*, 2004) and Belgium (Vanden Auweele *et al.*, 2008). As with studies of sexual abuse in general, comparisons between these studies are difficult due to variations in definitions of abuse and harassment, sampling and response rates. With regard to the last, Brackenridge (2001) warned that surveys with low response rates must be approached with caution as they may over-represent survivors and under-represent non-victims.

Factors associated with sexual harm in sport

Prior research has identified factors associated with sexual harm in sport, although specific causal factors have not been identified. Although there are too few systematically recorded data on sexual harm in sport to identify any statistically significant risk factors, tentative 'clusters' of risks have been extrapolated from interview data (Brackenridge and Kirby, 1997; Brackenridge, 2001; Cense and Brackenridge, 2001).

The risk of child sexual abuse appears to increase just before young elite athletes reach their best performance level, also known as the 'stage of imminent achievement' (Brackenridge and Kirby, 1997).

Brackenridge and Kirby (ibid.) suggest this is the period where athletes have most at stake in their sporting careers. Sports careers peak at different ages depending on the sport, with the highest levels of competitive performance ranging from teenage years to adulthood. Recognition of this has led to the coining of 'sport age' or age relative to peak performance in a particular sport, rather than chronological age. This concept allows for comparisons on the basis of potential peak performance, for differently aged athletes, and between athletes of the same sex (ibid., p. 411). Cense and Brackenridge (2001) suggest athletes in sports with young ages of imminent achievement may be especially vulnerable to risk of sexual abuse.

Several studies indicate that aspects of elite level sport may present the greatest risk of sexual abuse: for example, the intensity of training regimes, travel and overnight stays (Kirby *et al.*, 2000; Leahy *et al.*, 2002; Fasting *et al.*, 2004). However, there is limited research examining the experiences of the majority of young athletes who participate in sport at lower levels.

Knowledge of the extent of sexual harm is closely linked to how far people who have experienced it feel able to disclose, either in childhood or adulthood. Many children do not tell anyone at the time of the abuse, and some never do. The NSPCC's prevalence study found only 28% of young adults (aged eighteen to twenty-four) who had experienced sexual abuse as a child told someone at the time, a further 27% told someone later, but 31% had never told anyone (Cawson *et al.*, 2000). Within sporting contexts, disclosure may be particularly difficult where the perpetrator is held in high regard, such as well-respected coaches or sporting officials (Hartill, 2009). Several cases, for example, came to light in the 1990s within British swimming, where high-ranking individuals abused multiple young athletes over decades before conviction (Myers and Barret, 2002).

Our own research was conducted within this context and it may be that sexual harm was under-reported. On the other hand, the survey was anonymous, completed online, and respondents could choose to fill it in privately. These circumstances may have increased the chances of disclosure. However, the numbers reporting sexual harm were small, and few who had experienced it came forward for interview, so findings in this area were tentative.

Taking account of the debates about definitions of, and boundaries between, sexual harassment and sexual harm, our research defined both by a set of behaviours (see glossary). The following sections look at each in turn.

Research participants' experience of sexual harassment

Twenty-nine per cent of participants in our study reported some experience of sexually harassing behaviour, making it the second most common form of harm in the research. Unsurprisingly, it was reported most commonly by young women — one-third of whom had experienced it — but it was also reported by 17% of young men. In examining the experience of young people who had been sexually harassed, the survey results were analysed in three categories: non-physical harassment; physical harassment; and other forms of harassment. These are discussed in turn, below.

Non-physical harassment

This was the most common form of harassment experienced by research participants and included the following behaviours: being subject to sexist jokes, being whistled or leered at and having sexual comments made about your appearance. More than 80% of those who reported sexual harassment had experienced at least one of these non-physical behaviours. This kind of harassment was more commonly experienced by young women than young men. Non-physical sexual harassment was a more common experience for those young people who competed at levels higher than recreational sport.

Being whistled and leered at, reported by 61% of respondents who were sexually harassed, was the most common of the non-physical behaviours. This was followed by being subject to sexist jokes (53%) and having sexual comments made about their appearance (38%). All of these behaviours increased with the level of competition. Being whistled and leered at and being subject to sexist jokes were more commonly experienced by young women than young men, but having sexual remarks made about your appearance was experienced by equal proportions of young men and women.

Physical harassment

This included: having your space invaded; physical contact that made you uncomfortable; being touched in a way that made you uncomfortable; and having a massage or rub that made you uncomfortable. Four in ten of those reporting sexual harassment had experienced at least one of these behaviours. Perhaps surprisingly, they were more commonly reported by young men than young women. Young people reported these behaviours at all levels of competition but they were more common at recreational level.

Having your space invaded was by far the most common of these physical sexually harassing behaviours. Thirty-five per cent of young people reporting harassment had experienced this in broadly similar proportions of young men and women. More active physical harassment was much rarer. Sixteen per cent reported physical contact that made them feel uncomfortable, and 8% of those reporting harassment had been touched during instruction in a way that made them uncomfortable. Three per cent (forty-nine respondents) said they had had a massage or rub that made them uncomfortable.

Other forms of harassment

The research also sought to determine whether young people had experienced sexually harassing behaviour involving phone calls, letters, emails and texts; or if they had received invitations to be alone with someone that had made them feel uncomfortable. Overall, 5% of people reporting sexual harassment experienced these types of behaviour. The most common of these experiences was receiving invitations to be alone with someone that made you uncomfortable, experienced by fewer than 1%.

Research participants' experience of sexual harm

Overall, 3% of respondents to the survey reported some form of sexually harmful behaviour in either their main or second sport. The behaviours included in this category were: being forced to kiss someone; having someone expose themselves to you; being touched sexually against your will; someone attempting to have sex with you against your will; and being forced to have penetrative sex. Perhaps surprisingly, young men were more likely to report sexual harm than young women — a finding that may be explained by the specific behaviours reported. Eighty per cent of those reporting sexual harm had had someone expose themselves — an experience more common among boys than girls. Types of sexual harm involving physical contact were rarely reported in the survey.

PHYSICAL HARM

In general, in contrast to emotional and sexual harm, acknowledgement of the physical harm of children has a long history in the UK. Concern about cruelty to children in the nineteenth century led to the establishment of the NSPCC. In more recent times, the 1960s brought recognition of 'battered child syndrome' and the death of Maria Colwell at the hands of her stepfather in the 1970s led to growing public concern (Creighton, 2002). Subsequent high-profile deaths of children at the hands of people expected to care for them have kept the issue in the public eye.

Although the physical abuse of children has been the focus of empirical investigation more generally (Cawson *et al.*, 2000), large-sample empirical studies of physical abuse within sporting environments are scarce. This is not to say that physical violence does not occur. Allegations of physical abuse made up 23% of 132 abuse allegations made to the Football Association over a three-year period (Brackenridge *et al.*, 2005).

Our study provided new insights into the nature of physical harm to children in sport in the UK. Twenty-four per cent of participants reported that they had experienced at least one of the behaviours that defined physical harm in either their main or second sport. After emotional harm and sexual harassment, it was the third most common form of harm reported in the survey and was more commonly reported by young men than young women.

When examining physical harm within sporting contexts, it is useful to distinguish between physical abuse directly perpetrated by adults and/or peers, and harm that occurs owing to the norms of sporting culture, or accidental injuries sustained as a result of the inherent physicality of the sport. This was a distinction some respondents were keen to draw, and it is explored in greater detail in the following chapters. Below, we consider physical harm under two headings: training through injury and exhaustion; and physical violence and aggression.

Training through injury or exhaustion

Being forced to train on when injured or exhausted was by far the most commonly reported physically harmful behaviours explored. Two-thirds of those who had been physically harmed said they had been forced to train on in their main sport when injured or exhausted. Young women were more likely to report that they had been forced to train on when injured or exhausted. The higher young people advanced through the competitive ranks, the more likely they were to report being forced to train on when injured or exhausted.

Physical aggression and violence

In addition to experiences of over-training and training through injury, we also gathered information about experiences of more active physical harm. Two-thirds of respondents who reported physical harm had experienced some aggressive treatment in sport. Included in 'aggressive treatment' were: being shoved; being shaken; being thrown about; being knocked down; having something thrown at you; and being forcefully restrained. The most common of these was being shoved, and young men were more likely to report aggressive treatment in both their main and second sports than young women.

Twenty-two per cent of those who reported physical harm had experienced more violent behaviours. Included within this category were: being hit with an open hand; being hit with a fist; being hit with an implement; being grabbed around the neck; and being beaten up. Being hit with a fist and being hit with an implement were the most commonly reported violent behaviours in our survey, and young men were more likely than young women to report experiencing violent treatment in their sports.

EMOTIONAL HARM

Existing evidence suggested that emotional harm may be the most prevalent form of child maltreatment, although it has received relatively little attention in the research and clinical literature compared to other forms of harm (Cawson *et al.*, 2000; Evans, 2002). Research on emotional harm has largely focused on families, rather than institutional contexts. Indeed, research on emotional harm in sport has only recently begun to emerge, and it has tended to focus on elite athletes (Gervis and Dunn, 2004; Stirling and Kerr, 2008).

Emotional harm was by far the most common type of harm experienced by our research participants, with 75% reporting having experienced it. Overall differences by gender were minimal but emotional harm was more commonly experienced by those competing at higher than recreational level. Nevertheless, even at a recreational level, two-thirds of respondents said that they experienced some form of emotionally harmful behaviour in their main sport.

Most commonly reported was being criticised about performance. Seventy-nine per cent of respondents who had experienced emotional harm said that they had been criticised about their performance. Being embarrassed or humiliated about something was almost as common, being reported by 77%. Sixty-six per cent reported being teased and 51% said they were shouted or sworn at. In the next few sections we examine some of the most common emotionally harmful behaviours explored in the survey in more detail.

Being criticised about performance

Young men were more likely to report being criticised about their performance than young women, but both were equally likely to say they experienced it regularly. Linked to this gender split is the fact that respondents were more likely to report this behaviour in football and rugby than in any of the other top seven sports in our survey.

Criticism about something to do with their performance can be a perfectly valid part of training and competition, and some participants in the research argued that the criticism they received was aimed at improving their performance and was generally constructive. However, there were also circumstances where criticism about performance was unhelpful, disproportionate and in some cases counter-productive. Existing research has highlighted the extent to which abusive coaching behaviours are commonplace in elite child sport (Gervis and Dunn, 2004; Stirling and Kerr, 2008). Evidence from our own research suggested that a critical sporting culture can be a feature of young athletes' experience even at a recreational level.

Nearly two-thirds of respondents who competed at recreational level in their main sport had been criticised about their performance — 12% regularly. Criticism of performance as part of a pattern of humiliation in coaching emerged on a number of occasions in the interviews and will be discussed in greater detail in Chapter 3.

Being shouted or sworn at

Closely linked to being criticised for your performance was being shouted and sworn at, which was mentioned by more than half of respondents who reported experiencing emotionally harmful behaviour. It was more commonly reported by young men than young women and by young people competing at higher levels in sport.

In general, respondents taking part in team sports (rugby, football, netball and hockey) were more likely to report that they were shouted and sworn at than participants in more individual sports (athletics, swimming, dance).

Being embarrassed or humiliated about something and being teased

Seventy-seven per cent of research participants who reported emotional harm had been embarrassed or humiliated about something in either their main or second sport, with dancers being more likely to report this treatment than participants in any of the other top seven sports. Being embarrassed or humiliated was almost as commonly experienced as being criticised for their performance, and interview data suggested that the two were closely linked. Being teased in the context of sport was also common, particularly among players of team sports, and was experienced by two-thirds of all those who mentioned emotional harm. There were minor variations in the extent to which young athletes reported that they were embarrassed or humiliated or teased according to the level at which they competed, though the upward trend as athletes advanced through the ranks was less marked here than in other aspects of emotional harm.

Being bullied

Overall, one-third of young people who reported emotional harm said they had been bullied. Bullying had been experienced by equal proportions of young men and women and appeared to be experienced more by young people participating in individual sports such as athletics and dance than by those taking part in team sports.

We also explored behaviours that may form part of a pattern of bullying. More than one-third of those reporting emotional harm said that they had been called names; 19% had had lies and rumours spread about them; and 39% said they had been ignored in a way that made them feel bad.

CONCLUSION

This chapter has given an overview of the various types of harm children can be exposed to while participating in organised sport. It has shown that while research has tended to focus on more serious forms of harm such as sexual harm and serious physical harm, our own research has indicated that emotionally harmful treatment may be experienced by the majority of children taking part in sport, from those competing recreationally, right through to international competition. A picture of widespread, disrespectful and potentially harmful treatment of young athletes emerged.

Many of the behaviours discussed in this chapter, if they were experienced exclusively between children might be dismissed as part of the cut and thrust of growing up. However, our research explicitly considered the experience of children in organised settings, where they were under the care and instruction of adults, and it raises questions about the role of adults in organised sport in fostering a more positive sporting culture for children.

The next chapter looks more closely at the issue of sporting culture and discusses the ways in which children competing in organised sport learn quickly to accept the norms of sport and to tolerate behaviours and experiences that, if experienced in other arenas, would be unacceptable.

CHAPTER 3

Sporting cultures

Introduction

In this chapter we explore the culture within the sports clubs where young people in our study spent their time. We start by introducing the notion of the 'sport ethic' — an over-arching principle of sporting participation — and we explore and extend this concept in relation to our own research with young adults. We then consider how the sport ethic may combine with specific characteristics of individual sports to create differing sporting cultures and suggest that some cultures may be more harmful to children than others.

THE SPORT ETHIC

Experiencing pain and injury are a normal part of participation in organised sport and ignoring injuries and 'playing through pain' are central principles of sporting culture. Research with athletes has highlighted normative values concerning athleticism, also termed the 'sport ethic' (Killick, 2009; Malcolm, 2006; Coakley, 2007). Athletes who adhere to the sport ethic tolerate pain and continue to compete while injured in order to maintain their athletic identities, to avoid negative sanctions and to win the respect of their team mates and coaches by demonstrating their commitment to the sport (Malcolm, 2006). Various people may play a role in maintaining athletes' devotion to the norms of sport, including parents, coaches, trainers, physicians, sports commentators, team mates and other athletes (Malcolm, 2006). This may be done by overtly exerting pressure on athletes to play in spite of an injury; providing painkillers and temporary remedies; imposing sanctions on athletes who sit out a competition because of an injury; or by glorifying the actions of athletes who play with pain (Malcolm, 2006).

Commenting on the relatively large and growing body of sociological research on pain and injury in sport, Malcolm (2006, pp. 496–7) argues that literature to date had focused on athletes, often those at elite level, who have already internalised the norms of the sport ethic:

> Athletes who show their gritty determination by playing through the pain are cultural heroes. But these heroes are not born; they are made. Their callous attitudes toward even extreme pain are the result of cultural messages that are reinforced throughout their sporting careers. But athletes do not necessarily start out with this attitude. Many young athletes participating in recreational youth sports enter the sporting world unaware of the sport ethic, and only after they begin competing do they begin to learn the brazen approach to pain that it demands.

This culture can have serious consequences for young athletes. Research about children participating in competitive sport who undergo intensive training at a young age suggests it can have serious implications for athletes' physical, physiological and psychological health (Maffulli and Pintore, 1990; American Academy of Pediatrics, 2000; David, 2005), and over-use injuries and burnout among young athletes have been identified as a growing problem in the US (Brenner, 2007).

Our study provided information about how the sport ethic operates and is maintained by both coaches and peers, using a mix of sanctions and guilt. Young people interviewed explained how they came to accept a culture where training through discomfort, injury and exhaustion was seen as normal and acceptable. It was a culture in which the rights of the child, and in particular the fundamental UNCRC principle of 'the best interests' of the child, often took second place to the demands of the sport and the needs of the team.

In some circumstances, the effects of training through injury seemed relatively minor and were described as being so by research participants.

One young woman, part of a recreational swimming club, described how her coach forced her to swim through the pain of cramp, saying that this was the best thing for her muscles. She acknowledged this might have an element of truth in it but, looking back, she thought to force her to carry on was inappropriate at the level at which she was competing. However, her remarks suggested she might have found this treatment acceptable had she been competing at a higher level, and that she accepted the tenets of the sport ethic.

Sometimes, however, coaches encouraged children to play through injury in a way that could have been dangerous.

A rugby player described how during a game he had been hit on the nose with an elbow, which had dazed him, and he thought he was suffering from moderate concussion. His coach told him to play on and he would be fine. The rugby player remembered that the coach in question did not have sufficient medical training to assess the injury but based his judgement on the fact that a couple of players had already come off the pitch with injuries, and to lose another player would have injured the chances of the team. The same rugby player went on to explain that, although he thought things were managed well at his rugby club, he and his team mates were under pressure to play when injured, and that injury was seen as a sign of weakness:

> I'd have said everything on the rugby side of things was fairly well managed. If you got an injury, you were checked out. If you wanted to play, you could play on. The only one, the only possible thing I could think of, is sort of rushing you back in to playing, probably marginally too early after injury. There's one of my mates who was always, always injuring his hamstring. No matter how much he stretched off, he would always pull it. Which is a bit of a bummer being a two-metre runner, it doesn't exactly help. But he always did this and the coach was always nagging him to try and get back fit, to stop being a girl and get into the game again. (*Young man: main sport rugby*)

The experience of a young archer was also illustrative of how the sport ethic operates even when not actively promulgated by coaches. He described competing with a broken finger following a fall. It was difficult for his coach to find a substitute for the competition so, despite his coach saying he did not have to compete, he took the decision to do so, in order to support the team. Looking back, despite the fact that he experienced no long-term ill effects, he thought it had been a risky thing to do.

Another young man described how he continued to play on in a rugby match in a way he now recognised as potentially dangerous:

> I remember like hurting my neck a bit and playing the front row, so at no point should I have been allowed to play on even if I felt ok to do so [but I did play on] ... At the time I wanted to come back on, but on reflection now as I am older, obviously I would still want to play on but I would hope that someone would pull me back and say no, don't do it, it could be risky. (*Young man: main sport rugby; second sport football*)

Looking back, he is clear that, although the sport ethic dictated that he should continue playing, an adult involved in his sport should have been taking a different view — one that protected his health and well-being.

As well as training while injured, some young people reported returning to training or competition too soon following an injury: for example, in circumstances that are described in greater detail in the next chapter, one young woman's early return to competitive kayaking following an injury resulted, ultimately, in her not being able to participate in her sport. Her experience was extreme, but the theme of acceptance of training through exhaustion and injury as normal recurred in the interviews, and was evident even at lower levels of competition.

The literature highlights a difficulty for coaches in distinguishing between intense training and over-training that may cause pain or injury. David (2005), arguing from a children's rights perspective, writes:

> A very thin line divides intensive training that allows children to fulfil themselves from that in which they are abused and exploited. It is not easy for adults to assess constantly whether the child's full development is benefiting or not from intensive training.

The examples above indicate that a difficulty also exists within competition even at lower levels. There is the danger that, for coaches and other adults, the best interests of the child can clash with the demands of the sport.

EXTENDING THE SPORT ETHIC

While the sport ethic tends to be understood in terms of athletes' relationship to pain and injury, the experience of research participants suggested that a culture of being uncomplaining about, and accepting of, a range of unpleasant experiences in sport was also part and parcel of the sport ethic for children involved in organised sport.

Respondents who reported any kind of harmful treatment in the survey were asked to say which of the harms they experienced they considered to be the most serious; then answer some further questions about whether they had told anyone about what had happened. For the majority of them (93%) the most serious harm was emotional harm. Fifty-nine per cent of those had never told anyone about the emotionally harmful experiences they had while taking part in sport. A similar proportion of the 1% who said sexual harassment was the most serious harm they experienced never told anyone. The 4% who said that physical harm was the most serious harm they experienced were a little more likely to have told someone about it but even amongst this group 47% had never told anyone about the harm they experienced.

When asked to explain why they did not tell anyone about the harmful treatment they had been subjected to, the most common reasons were to do with respondents' own judgements about the seriousness of the incidents described. 'It wasn't a big deal', 'it was only minor', 'it didn't really upset me much', 'it was just a bit of banter between team mates', 'it wasn't important enough' were all common responses to this question. Other responses mentioned 'not wanting to make a fuss', and the importance of dealing with your own problems yourself.

Interviews allowed young people to explain in more detail the extent to which they expected and accepted disrespectful, hurtful and harmful treatment without complaint.

A young man described his experience of feeling excluded by his peers on his athletics team. Part of the reason for this was that, although he enjoyed his sport, he was not as good as his peers — a fact that was frequently the subject of 'mocking, fake encouragement' from team mates. He explained his decision not to tell anyone by making reference to the culture of the sport:

> No, I wouldn't have ever talked about it but again it maybe wasn't
> a big deal. But in my mind it was just the way things were, the sort
> of natural order of things, you know, you had the sporty people who
> were always like this. (*Young man: main sport badminton; second
> sport athletics*)

The close personal relationships in recreational sport, where parents
were involved in running clubs, could also militate against telling
anyone about emotionally harmful treatment.

A young man, who reported a range of hurtful treatment from his peers regarding
both his sporting skill base and more personal issues, described why he chose not
to tell anyone about the way he was treated:

> I am quite a personal person so I tend to just like keep stuff inside.
> Because I loved playing rugby, I didn't want to like go to my parents
> or you know so and so said this, or did this. And like with the coach,
> it was generally like their sons who were having a pop in the first
> place, so you wouldn't go to them either. (*Young man: main sport
> rugby; second sport football*)

These young men, like other participants in our research, learned
through their experience in sport that they had to accept and deal
with difficult issues on their own and without complaint if they
wanted to continue to participate in the sports they loved, in the
same way as they learned to accept pain and injury.

Another young man described how players would get 'a bit of taunting' about
both 'flashy arrogance' in their play and about poor performance. He mentioned how
there was a lot of 'locker room banter' which could 'get a bit personal sometimes',
but it was all with a 'jokey' attitude'. His view was clear that this sort of behaviour
had to be accepted, and that it was unacceptable to complain about it:

> I don't think I ever ratted anyone out if they just said something.
> It was usually when they had done something like stolen my gear,
> or something like that. I didn't see the banter as a reason to go
> squealing to a coach. (*Young man: main sport ice hockey; second
> sport football*)

PARTICULAR SPORTING CULTURES

Previous literature suggested that the sport ethic operates to a greater or lesser extent across all sports. The experience of our research participants indicated, however, that there were particular sporting cultures in individual sports which exacerbated its effects.

Football and rugby were the most commonly played sport by male participants. They were also played by a small number of girls. Football had the highest reporting of emotional harm of the top seven sports and rugby the second highest. In the case of physical harm, rugby had the highest reporting, followed by football. Both also scored unexpectedly highly on sexual harassment and sexual harm, behaviours that, at interview, were revealed to consist largely of sexual 'banter' between team mates and sexualised behaviour such as flashing and behaviours such as 'bum grabbing' and forced kissing.

In both these sports, pressure to subjugate individual needs and wishes to those of the team was evident from the testimony of our research participants. Young men reported pressure to return to play 'for the good of the team' when they had been injured. While these pressures existed in other sports to a certain extent, the potential for injury was greater in these sports, particularly in rugby. Young men reported an encouragement to play aggressively, and one put it particularly vividly: 'it's basically fighting with a few rules'. Another young man highlighted the status aggressive behaviour could bring to players, although he was careful to note that it was not condoned by adults:

> Football culture is passionate and young children will have fights and get sent off. It's the kind of culture where your manager will tell you off for having the fight. But your team mates, they'll hold you in high esteem. It's almost glorifying and somehow is an extremely important experience. (*Young man: main sport football; second sport winter sports*)

This aggressive behaviour on the pitch was supported by a particular culture off it. As one participant noted:

> The shouting was done by the coaches to pretty much everyone in the team, and the teasing was done by my team

mates … I believe it is quite normal in a rugby club environment, and did not have problems with it then, and don't have them now. (*Young man: main sport rugby; second sport martial arts*)

A young footballer made a similar point: 'Teasing and name-calling are part of competitive sport, especially the more "alpha-male" sports such as football.' A rugby player argued that:

Shouting and being sworn at can be perceived in two different ways. It can be very mean that will emotionally harm a person. But in rugby, for example, being shouted and sworn at will make you more competitive and alert. (*Young man: main sport rugby; second sport martial arts*)

This notion that these behaviours were in some way inherent in these sports and could not be separated from them came up frequently in the research: for example, rugby players and footballers said that sexual remarks and jokes 'were part and parcel' of the game. The frequency with which these views emerged suggested that boys who play these sports quickly internalise the cultural norms within them.

Other team sports also had high rates of emotional and physical harm. However, in both football and rugby, the reporting of aggressive and violent treatment within the physical harm category was higher. There was also a particular issue in these sports with sexualised behaviour between male peers. Netball and hockey had high numbers reporting sexual harassment, but the profile of perpetrators of sexual harassment was different. In outdoor sports played by girls, particularly in netball, players were subject to leering, whistling and sexual remarks from passers-by and spectators. In rugby and football, the 'locker room' antics and sexual banter came from team mates and peers.

The issues with rugby and football appeared to be related to the fact that they were team sports, predominantly played by boys. Individual sports competed in mainly by girls also shared a similar culture. Dance was one of the top seven sports in the research and was the third most common amongst young women respondents.

Gymnastics was only the eleventh most popular sport overall but was eighth amongst girls, and shared certain characteristics with dance.

Research participants taking part in both dance and gymnastics reported emotional harm and physical harm at levels broadly in line with that of all respondents. Their experience of sexual harassment was lower than that of participants in other predominantly female sports such as hockey and netball. What makes these sports distinctive is the higher reporting of harm perpetrated by coaches and trainers than other sports, across all of these types of harm.

Amongst those who gave their main sport as dance, 73% of those reporting physical harm said their trainer or teacher was involved, by far the highest of our top seven sports. The equivalent figure for gymnastics was 52%, which is more in line with other individual sports such as swimming (58%) and athletics (50%) but considerably higher than in team sports such as football (22%) and netball (23%).

Coaches were also more likely to be the perpetrators of emotional harm in these sports. Amongst young people who gave their main sport as dance, 48% of those reporting emotional harm said their coach was involved. The figure for those reporting emotional harm while competing in gymnastics as their main sport was also 48%. Swimmers reported this at a similar level (43%) but the equivalent figure for netball was 22%.

Nearly three-quarters of main sport gymnasts who mentioned sexual harassment said that their coach was involved in the behaviours they reported. This was a far higher proportion than was the case for any of our top seven sports, although absolute numbers were small. Within the top seven sports, dance had the highest proportion of respondents saying their coach or trainer was involved in these behaviours.

The qualitative information in our survey provided more information on how these relationships worked. They presented a picture of intense relationships between gymnastic coaches and dance teachers and their students, coupled with gruelling training regimes, sometimes at very young ages.

A young dancer commented on the way in which teachers undermined their students:

> I think that when I look back it does seem like a lot of negative attitudes were around the dancing school. I know girls that left because of what the teachers said to them about their looks, weight or how they danced. (*Young man: main sport dance; second sport swimming*)

Gymnasts gave particularly vivid testimony about the way in which their coaches behaved. One commented: 'In gymnastics the coaches are very hard on you and will push your body beyond its physical limitations.' Another painted an even more disturbing picture: 'They would make you train through tears. They sealed up the windows so no parents could watch.'

In gymnastics, punishing regimes became even more intense as athletes competed at higher levels. One, who competed at national and international level, echoed the point made by the young gymnast above as she described training regimes built on humiliating and isolating gymnasts:

> I mean the whole training was like, if you do one thing wrong then suddenly like you are being screamed at in the middle of an entire gym whether there are five year olds in there, or just your team in there. You are pointed out, isolated out, whether it's sent out the gym or just like screamed at or laughed at in front of the entire club. (*Young woman: main sport gymnastics*)

A gymnast described the intense physical pressure that was put on young gymnasts and how it was linked to an implicit threat of being dropped from the squad:

> You know, the thing that was expected of us was that we'd always push ourselves that little bit further. And, you know, I do remember just coming out of sessions feeling absolutely drained beyond belief. And thinking 'god I'm completely drained, I couldn't ever do that again'. And yet I went back for more … I guess I felt responsible. You know, I, it was the sense of, you know, I, yes it was hard but I've got to keep going. If I still want my place in this then I'm going

to have to fight for it. And yeah I suppose a lot of kids would just say: 'I've had enough, I don't want to do any more, mum', but yeah I took it quite seriously.(*Young woman: main sport gymnastics; second sport equestrian sports*)

CONCLUSION

In this chapter we have introduced the notion of the sport ethic and discussed the way in which individual sporting cultures are built on it. Early in their sporting lives, young people learn that success and affirmation in sport are gained through adhering to the norms of sport in general and their own sport in particular. This process teaches them to accept pain and discomfort, as well as disrespectful, hurtful and emotionally harmful treatment. In the following chapters we expand on these themes to explore the roles of coaches, other adults and peers in the harmful treatment of children in sport.

CHAPTER 4

Coaches and other adults as perpetrators of disrespectful and harmful treatment of children

Introduction

A fundamental lesson from research on child maltreatment in general is that most abuse is perpetrated by someone the child knows and trusts. Gervis and Dunn (2004) note the importance of the coach–athlete relationship for child elite athletes. They further observe that child athletes are training longer and harder, and spend more time with coaches, and may perceive the relationship as a more important one than that with their parents. In addition, coaches at elite level have investment in athletes which may relate to their own career advancement. This can lead to a potential vulnerability of child athlete to coach if their influence is misused: 'Competitive sport is usually based on an unbalanced relationship of power between trainers and athletes, which is even more apparent when it comes to youngsters, and empowerment is rarely valued' (David, 2005, p. 84).

Farstad (2007) notes the potential for abuse and violence in competitive sport when young athletes spend a great deal of time with their coaches and other adults, away from their parents. This is particularly the case when children travel to competitions and spend nights away from home at tournaments and competitions.

These factors find echoes in Cense and Brackenridge's work (2001) outlining risk factors for sexual harassment and sexual abuse relating to a coach. They note that coaches were likely to be male, older, well-respected within the club and community, with accredited qualifications, a high degree of trust from parents and with any previous record of sexual crimes unknown. Other risk factors include opportunities to be alone with athletes in training, at their home or at competitions and trips away.

Coaches and other adults involved in organised sport for children are important authority figures in their athletes' lives and sometimes spend a great deal of time with them. In the context of children's rights, they have a clear role in promoting the best interests of the child. This will include looking after their health and physical well-being, ensuring their views are taken into account, and ensuring they are protected from physical and mental neglect and abuse. More generally, Article 5 of the UN Convention concerns the right to appropriate guidance from adults, 'consistent with the evolving capacities of the child'.

OVERVIEW OF COACHES AND OTHER ADULTS AS PERPETRATORS OF HARM

Table 4.1 shows the proportions of young people who reported various types of harm in our survey and gave their coach or trainer as a perpetrator of the harm. As the table shows, coaches were implicated in physical and emotional harm by approximately one-third of respondents experiencing those types of harm in both their main and second sports. In the case of both physical and emotional harm, young women were more likely to cite their coaches as perpetrators than young men. Coaches were mentioned as perpetrators in the case of 21% of those experiencing sexual harassment in their main sport, in broadly similar proportions of young men and women. Coaches had a more minor role in the sexually harmful treatment of young people in our survey, although, as we saw in Chapter 2, absolute numbers experiencing sexual harm were small.

Table 4.1: Percentage of respondents giving team coaches/trainers as perpetrators of various types of harm in main and second sport, by gender.

	Main sport			Second sport		
	Total	Male	Female	Total	Male	Female
Emotional harm	34%	29%	36%	33%	27%	35%
Physical harm	37%	28%	41%	31%	26%	33%
Sexual harassment	21%	21%	21%	24%	26%	24%
Sexual harm	8%	5%	11%	9%	9%	9%

Note: More than one answer was possible

The role of coaches as perpetrators of all types of harm showed an upward trend as young athletes advanced through the competitive ranks. Team mates and peers were the most frequently cited perpetrators in all types of harm, and this is discussed in greater detail in the next chapter. In the cases of emotional harm, sexual harassment and sexual harm, team mates and peers remain the most frequently cited perpetrators at all levels. However, at national and international level, coaches overtake peers as the most frequently named perpetrators of physical harm.

Young people participating in individual sports were generally more likely than those competing in team sports to name their coaches as perpetrators: for example, 73% of young people who had been physically harmed while doing dance as their main sport said their coach was involved. Swimming (58%) and athletics (50%) also had high proportions of young people giving their coach or trainer as a perpetrator of the physical harm they reported. By contrast, less than a quarter (19%) of young people reporting physical harm while doing hockey as their main sport said their coach or trainer was involved. Similar proportions were given for those competing in football (22%), rugby (23%) and netball (23%).

A similar pattern was evident for young people reporting emotional harm, with coaches more frequently cited as perpetrators in individual sports than team sports. For example, of those who reported emotional harm in their main sport, 48% of dancers and 43% of swimmers said their coach or trainer was involved in the emotional harm they experienced compared to 22% of netball players and 27% of footballers.

Although the numbers reporting sexual harm by coaches were too small to observe meaningful variations in their incidence according to type of sport, reporting of coach or trainer perpetrated sexual harassment was also more common in individual than team sports. However, sexual harassment showed some interesting features when 'other' perpetrators were examined. Table 4.2 shows the proportion of respondents giving 'other adult in club' and 'other' as a person responsible for the harm they experienced. The role of adults in clubs (other than coaches) in the harm of the research participants was considerably lower than the role of coaches, with 8% and less saying that another club adult was involved in the harm they experienced in their main sport. As with coaches, the extent to which participants reported the involvement of other adults in the club as responsible for the harm they

Table 4.2: Percentage of respondents giving 'other adult in club' and 'other' as perpetrators of various types of harm in main sport, by gender.

	Other adult in club			Other		
	Total	Male	Female	Total	Male	Female
Emotional harm	6%	7%	6%	5%	6%	5%
Physical harm	3%	4%	3%	11%	11%	11%
Sexual harassment	8%	7%	8%	21%	14%	22%
Sexual harm	6%	3%	8%	7%	5%	8%

experienced showed an upward trend as young people advanced to the higher levels of competition, but there was little variation by sport in their involvement in harm.

When the role of 'other' perpetrators was examined, some interesting issues emerged. The most striking figure here is that over a fifth of young people who reported experiencing sexual harassment in their main sport said that an 'other' person was responsible, an experience considerably more frequently reported by young women than young men. It is not possible from the data to specify exactly which people constitute the 'other' category. However, when the figures are examined by main sport, those showing the highest levels of 'other'-perpetrated sexual harassment were sports primarily played by girls outside (netball and hockey) suggesting that the sexual harassment of girls by spectators and passers-by is an issue for these sports. This is considered in greater detail later in this chapter.

COACHES, PHYSICAL HARM AND INSTILLING THE SPORT ETHIC

The previous chapter introduced the notion of the sport ethic, the process by which young athletes learn to accept pain and injury as an integral part of participating in sport. The evidence of young participants in our research affirmed the key role of coaches in this process through an encouragement to train excessively or to train through injury and exhaustion. The role of coaches in physical harm is particularly important because, as noted above, in contrast to other forms of harm, they become the most frequent source of physical harm to child athletes who compete at national and international level.

Young people did not appear to consider what they experienced to be harmful, so long as it occurred while they were supervised by a coach or a trainer. And, in some circumstances reported by research participants, training while exhausted may have been under careful control and fairly benign in its impacts. A young man who competed in football at local level and tennis at district level explained:

> Being trained while exhausted was always under supervision by the coach/trainer, so it wasn't anything like a physical harm, but more like training harder to achieve better results, which actually helped without harming me in any way. (*Young man: main sport football; second sport tennis*)

The following comment, however, indicated that there were circumstances in which the norms of sporting culture take precedence over the welfare of athletes, despite the incident being minimised by the young woman concerned, who competed at district level in equestrian sports:

> I had an asthma attack while riding and my instructor wouldn't let me use my medication which I was upset about at the time but I managed to carry on and I actually achieved what she wanted me to and felt better after. It just seemed a bit unfair to push me like that. (*Young woman: main sport equestrian sports; second sport badminton*)

It is arguable that this young woman's trainer breached her rights in a serious way. She failed to listen to her views and potentially risked her physical health by refusing to allow her to take her medication while she suffered an asthma attack. Despite this, the young woman commented that she felt better because she had achieved what she wanted her to achieve — an indication of the power and influence coaches can have over their athletes.

The experience of one of the research participants, shown in the case study below, was a vivid example of the power and influence of coaches and of the temptations they may be under to use this influence in contravention of their athletes' rights, particularly when competitive success and career advancement are at stake.

A club swimmer, between the ages of eight and twelve, competed at district level. After swimming, she joined the sea cadets where she began kayaking. Her talent for the sport was soon identified and she began racing, ultimately competing nationally.

She experienced physical harm in both her sports. In swimming, her coach would make her and her fellow swimmers train so hard they were sometimes physically sick in the pool through exertion: 'You know, they might have to stop to fish out the sick, but that was literally it'. Her coach would tell her that if she didn't train hard she would not be able to race for the club at the weekend, and she completely believed that if she stopped before the end of the session she would never be good enough. This was a terrible threat, because swimming was the most important thing in her life. She had given up her other social activities; she trained sixteen hours a week, and the only things in her life were swimming and school work.

The coaches at her club had all been elite swimmers — 'they were top, top coaches' — and their aim was to coach elite swimmers. Missing training was not an option, whatever the circumstances. When she contracted glandular fever, her doctor said she shouldn't swim for six weeks, but her coach said that if she did not return to swimming after two weeks, she would never be able to compete for the club again. This young woman begged her mum to take her, and her mum agreed, after extracting a promise that she would get out of the pool if she felt ill: 'And I would always just carry on kind of thing, you know, you have to.'

Finally, despite her protests, her mum made her leave swimming because she could see that it was making her unhappy and was not a positive experience for her. This young woman was relieved, as she didn't want to stay but it was difficult for her to make that clear: 'I couldn't wait to leave so I was quite pleased to have someone else to blame for it. My mum doesn't want me to do it any more, it's not my fault.'

After leaving swimming, she soon became involved in kayaking, a sport she loved. She found the atmosphere much more fun and supportive than she had at swimming and she enjoyed the boisterousness of training sessions. She was also good at it, winning races at district level and catching the eye of national coaches by the time she was fifteen. At around this time she tore a ligament in her shoulder and, she now thinks, went back to competitive racing too soon. She could feel that something was wrong and spoke to her coaches and consulted sports physiotherapists. Between them, it was agreed that she could carry on for two years and try to be the best she could, or she could leave the club and not return. Given that choice, she decided to carry on, with the result that she developed a back injury that prevented her from kayaking beyond the age of eighteen.

She thinks now that she should have been encouraged to keep her fitness levels up through swimming and recreational kayaking but shouldn't have been allowed to go back to competition until her injury had properly healed. She thinks her coaches had issues other than her best interests in mind:

> The national coaches would end up getting reward money for the amount that the team, the amount of gold the team would take home. I was one of the gold racers, one of the ones more likely to get a gold. When I got my injury my national coach wanted me to race to get the credit. So it was quite selfish of them … I should never have been allowed to have played. (*Young woman: main sport kayaking; second sport swimming*)

PHYSICAL AGGRESSION AND VIOLENCE FROM COACHES

In establishing a conceptual framework for researching maltreatment in sport, Stirling (2008) notes that physical abuse incorporates both contact and non-contact physical abuse, and presents (hypothetical) examples of different forms of physical abuse of children within sporting contexts. Contact physical abuse might involve punching, beating, kicking, biting, shoving, striking, shaking, throwing, stabbing, choking, burning, spanking, slapping, whacking, hitting with a stick, strap or other object. Non-contact physical abuse might involve: washing an athlete's mouth out with soap; requiring an athlete to remain motionless or in a seated position without a chair; forcing an athlete to kneel on a harmful surface; isolation in a confined space; denying use of the toilet; denying access to needed water, food or sleep; and forced physical exertion.

Some of these practices echo coaching behaviours that have been reported anecdotally. David (2005, p. 69) discusses accounts of the corporal punishment of young athletes from a range of countries, including the United States, Switzerland and Germany, noting:

> Though specific research is still scant, corporal punishment is sometimes inflicted in the sports world on young athletes who do not perform as well as expected and on those who do not conform to the strict discipline.

In our research, few instances of physical aggression and violence by coaches were reported by research participants. However, when physical aggression and violence were reported it was used as a means of control or punishment, sometimes concealed as accidental or instructional: for example, a young woman who had been involved in equestrian sports as a child described how 'once in a while' her instructor would catch her leg with the riding crop she used on the horses. Although this was presented as though it was accidentally done when trying to discipline the horse, the young woman thought it was deliberate.

As with coaches sometimes encouraging their athletes to over-train or train through injury, violent and aggressive behaviour occasionally arose as a result of their expectations not being met and their frustration and anger not being kept in check. The experience of an international gymnast illustrates this:

> Being little, if you are standing on top of a beam and you do something wrong, like the coach gets angry, or it's one of your worst coaches or whatever, but they usually just shove you and push you off the beam completely, like irrelevant of whether you hurt yourself on the floor, you are off and you are down and you are out the gym. I mean again it does take quite a while, it's not move wrong and you're off, if you try a move a few times and you just can't get the hang of it, they get wound up and then it's lashing out. And I think the worst thing for me, obviously you're always shaken about, always thrown about and stuff, just to kind of, I don't know, lash out again. (*Young woman: main sport gymnastics*)

These examples of physical punishment by coaches, while not common, are clearly unacceptable from a children's rights perspective. Article 19 of the Convention enshrines the right of children to be protected from physical and mental violence, and, more generally, the Convention states that the best interests of children should be paramount in any situation involving them. The evidence from young people in this and other research showed that coaches' own interests can also influence their treatment of the young athletes they train.

EMOTIONAL HARM AS A COACHING TOOL

Research evidence indicates emotionally abusive coaching behaviours are commonly experienced by elite child athletes, with more abusive behaviours reported as they advanced through the ranks (Gervis and Dunn, 2004; Stirling and Kerr, 2007; Stirling and Kerr, 2008). Although athletes rarely use the term 'emotional abuse', they express distress as the result of a range of coaching behaviours (Stirling and Kerr, 2007). One qualitative UK study (Gervis and Dunn, 2004) with twelve former elite child athletes found all reported being frequently shouted at, with belittling, threats and humiliation also commonplace. Half the participants said they were ignored or rejected, and one-third said their coaches isolated them. Drawing on the qualitative accounts of fourteen Canadian former elite youth female swimmers, Stirling and Kerr (2008) identify three types of emotionally abusive coach behaviours: physical, verbal and the denial of attention/support. Reported physical behaviours included: throwing objects either at, or in the presence of, an athlete; punching walls; and breaking training equipment when frustrated with an athlete's performance. Verbal behaviours included yelling, shouting, belittling, name-calling, humiliation and degrading comments, including inappropriate comments about weight and physical appearance. While athletes reported negative responses to such verbal behaviours and physical demonstrations of anger, it was the denial of attention and support, which included being ignored, being expelled or excluded from practice, which was described as the most negatively experienced type of emotionally abusive coaching behaviour.

Former child athletes' responses to their coaches' abusive behaviour were similar across both studies, with descriptions of feeling stupid, worthless, upset, angry, guilty, depressed, humiliated, fearful, hurt, inferior and lacking in self-confidence. Stirling and Kerr (2007) examined elite athletes' experiences of emotional abuse over the course of their career, noting that, while such coaching behaviours might be accepted as a necessary part of the elite sport culture at the outset, emotionally abusive coach behaviour may be experienced more negatively as an athlete perceives his or her performance to be deteriorating. Gervis and Dunn (2004, p. 221) highlight the implications of these emotional responses for athletes' performance, suggesting a 'destructive cycle' in which athletes' deteriorating performance leads to an intensification of abusive coaching behaviour. However, despite the negative impact on elite child athletes, Gervis and Dunn (2004, pp. 220–2) argue that these coaching behaviours are habitual:

> No one seems to question such coaching behaviour; it is accepted as being part of sport, and often takes place behind closed doors ... The elite child athlete has to cope with pressures of training, long hours and competing at the highest level in a climate of sustained attacks on their self-esteem at a time when they are most vulnerable ... This behaviour goes on without being challenged or questioned so long as the athlete is successful. This contributes to the habitual coaching tools and creates a culture of coaching which reinforces those behaviours that are associated with success.

These practices at elite level were mirrored by the experiences of the young people in our study who had participated as elite child athletes. These young people spoke of a pattern of humiliation and belittling in coaching practice. The example below comes from a young woman who competed at district level in gymnastics, leaving the sport by the time she was twelve, at the point at which she was being considered for the national squad.

> Yeah, no, again there were certain coaches that really hated you, and they had favourites and if you were flawed in any way they would take that out immediately. So if you were a little over-weight you were called chubby and that would be a nickname from coaches and stuff. And then general humiliation and like if you did one thing wrong it was really like pointed out, and really kind of exaggerated in front of everyone. Like there was no way you were going to get away with it kind of thing. Or if you argued back, or anything, like everything was so dramatic and such a huge scene and really kind of over-done in a way. But it really isolated one person, or whoever it was who was in the wrong at the time.
> (*Young woman: main sport gymnastics*)

The experience of the young gymnast above took place in the context of training for high-level competition. However, research participants who competed at lower levels also reported emotionally harmful treatment being a routine part of coaching practice.

One young man, who competed in ice hockey at club level, explained how his coaches used public-humiliation embarrassment as a training tool, to put someone in their place:

> We had a competition in training called … we called it juice boy basically, just a penalty shoot-out and the loser has to wear a pretty pink helmet the next time they go on the ice. There was one occasion where the goalies were told [by the coach] to let everybody score except this one kid. (*Young man: main sport ice hockey; second sport football*)

This level of organisation was unusual and the young man concerned described the particular circumstances of this case, in which coaches enlisted the support of the young athletes in their charge to humiliate a team mate, as only happening once. However, the practice of conducting a penalty shoot-out in which the player with the poorest performance would have to wear a pink helmet was described as a routine 'bit of fun … but also a training tool' for the end of most training sessions.

No other research participants described situations in which coaches and teams worked in concert to humiliate, but public humiliation in the context of training was far from uncommon. Participants spoke of being given public punishments for poor performance, such as being made to join the class for younger children, or being made to do exercises or laps on their own but in front of others.

We saw in Chapter 2 that more than half of the young people who had experienced emotionally harmful treatment while competing in organised sport had been shouted and sworn at, 12% of them regularly. Evidence from research participants showed that being shouted and sworn at by coaches could be upsetting, demoralising and, at times, humiliating.

A young rugby player described the impact of such emotionally harmful behaviour from a coach when he was under fourteen, and playing at local club level:

> Yeah, there was definitely times when you could have someone [one of the coaches] really having a go at you, to the point that like you'd be crying.

He went on to explain that criticism that could leave him or other players in tears was commonplace, occurring at least once a fortnight and that the impact was greater because the criticism would take place in front of the rest of the team in a way that could be humiliating. (*Young man: main sport rugby; second sport athletics*)

At higher levels of competition, the young people described coaches losing their temper to the point where they became irrational.

A swimmer, who competed for Scotland, explained what happened when his coach lost her temper:

> Sometimes it was quite relaxed, you could speak to her really easily and stuff, but then when she would get annoyed, I don't know, it was weird. She was different ... She would just swear at you and go mental, and her face would go bright red and storm off, and just wouldn't accept any sort of argument or reasoning at all.

In an echo of the findings of the Gervis and Dunn (2004) study, he went on to explain the impact this treatment had on how he felt about his sport in terms that indicated the counter-productive nature of such behaviour. He also indicated his understanding that it may have been driven by her personal investment in his success:

> It totally demotivates you, and sometimes like if you have been at a competition for like, sometimes it would be three days, like Friday, Saturday and Sunday, and you have not been doing particularly great, and then last thing on the Sunday you have to do this race, you have been knackered all weekend, you have done seven races or something, you put everything you have into it, and you only end up swimming like half a second more than what you would usually swim, so it was still a not bad swim. You would come out and she would go mental because you didn't get a PB [personal best], and she would honestly lose the plot, it would be like wasted my whole weekend, just don't bother coming to training on Monday, I can't be bothered. (*Young man: main sport swimming; second sport triathlon*)

Seen within a children's rights framework, the coaching practices revealed are questionable. It could be argued that the coaches who employed them failed to protect child athletes from practices that could be mentally, psychologically or emotionally abusive, and contravened Article 19 of the UN Convention. They also raise questions about the extent to which such practices could be called 'appropriate guidance', within the terms of Article 5 of the Convention.

SEXUAL HARASSMENT: CLOTHING, PASSERS-BY AND COMPLICITY

A key finding from our research noted above is the extent to which participants were exposed to sexual harassment. As we saw in Chapter 2, 29% of respondents and a higher proportion of girls had experienced some form of sexually harassing behaviour, most commonly whistling, leering and sexist comments and jokes.

As with other forms of harm, the most frequent perpetrators of sexually harassing behaviour were team mates and peers. As will be discussed in greater detail in the next chapter, a lot of girls tended to see these behaviours as 'boys being boys' and something that could be 'laughed off'.

It was noted above that coaches were less commonly cited by research participants as perpetrators of sexual harassment than of other types of harm explored in the research. However, some participants talked of coaches commenting on the appearance of young athletes, particularly girls. One girl involved in swimming and tennis described how, in tennis, coaches were very aware of girls' appearance and girls knew this. She described how coaches would tell girls if they looked good and would point out if they appeared to have lost weight or if their bottoms had got smaller — 'They knew your figure off by heart'. At the time she did not think much of it but looking back as an adult she thought it was 'perverted'.

Research examining adult, elite female athletes' experience of sexual harassment found that there were no significant differences in the level of harassment according to the amount of clothing worn for the sport (Fasting *et al.*, 2004). Our research participants, however, were reflecting on their experience as children and young people. They spoke of puberty as a time when sexually harassing behaviours began to emerge, a time when girls could be particularly self-conscious about looks and appearance as their bodies changed. In this context, they became aware of revealing sports gear such as swimming costumes, leotards and short skirts as a focal point for leering, sexual comments and jokes, sometimes from coaches, as above, but also from spectators and passers-by.

Well the club where we trained had huge fire doors in the middle of public areas and stuff, so you used to keep like all the doors open and like an entire club of like young girls in leotards for training. And so a lot of people came and watched, and lot of them were like younger guys and stuff. (*Young woman: main sport gymnastics*)

At netball, the courts were outside and near to the main road and passers-by used to wolf whistle but nothing more than that. We were prancing about in those little netball skirts. It made me feel uncomfortable. (*Young woman: main sport netball; second sport gymnastics*)

A young woman spoke of being uncomfortable when her swimming team had photographs taken in their swimming costumes when they taking part in competitions, because it focused on the bodies of the team in a way that she thought was unnecessary and inappropriate. Looking back, she was very clear that this should not have been allowed, and the adults involved in her sport should not have exposed her to this kind of experience.

Yeah I just, I don't see, even now looking back on it, why it's necessary to take photos of us whilst swimming or having us holding onto the bar smiling at the photographer in the swimming pool. There's no need for that kind of photograph. I don't know if it would be allowed now anyway. But why could the photos not be of us in our tracksuits winning the medals and things? That's the kind of appropriate time to do the photography. I don't see any need, everyone knows what swimming is. But if you want photos of the team take them in a team tracksuits. Don't take them of twelve-year-old girls, eleven-year-old girls in their swimming costumes. (*Young woman: main sport kayaking; second sport swimming*)

Even where coaches and other adults involved in the sports were not direct perpetrators of sexually harassing behaviour, some research participants thought they were complicit in it through their failure to tackle it and take it seriously, or even, like the young woman quoted above, by providing opportunities for it.

It was common for young women to speak of being outside in

clothing that made them uncomfortable because of the attention it brought them. If coaches and other adults witnessed the behaviour their responses fell into two categories: either they told the girls to ignore it, or they would move the perpetrators on. There was no evidence of approaches that directly tackled the behaviour: for example, by changing coaching practice by allowing girls to dress in a way that made them more comfortable; or by dealing with the behaviour of spectators and passers-by in anything more than a piecemeal way. Young women research participants looking back on their experience all spoke of this sort of behaviour as something they had to get used to and tolerate.

The same was true of adult responses to the leering and sexual remarks girls were subjected to by their peers. If witnessed, adults reprimanded perpetrators but this was always described as something that was done in a piecemeal way, and girls learned that they had to tolerate this behaviour as something that was part of their participation in organised sport.

Article 34 of the UN Convention concerns the right to protection from sexual exploitation and abuse. If, following Brackenridge (2001), sexual exploitation in sport is understood as a continuum encompassing all forms of unwanted sexual behaviour, the type of sexually harassing behaviour experienced by these research participants sits clearly along this spectrum, and something from which children should be protected.

CONCLUSION

This chapter has considered the role of adults, and especially coaches, as the perpetrators of harmful treatment of children. It has focused on three main areas: physical harm, emotional harm and sexual harassment. All three are explicitly considered within the UN Convention on the Rights of the Child: Article 19 concerns the right to protection from neglect and physical and mental violence, while Article 34 enshrines the right to protection from sexual exploitation.

More general rights of relevance to the relationship between adults and children involved in organised sport are the right of the child to appropriate guidance, and the over-arching principle within the Convention that the best interests of the child should be paramount.

Existing research evidence and the testimony of our research participants suggests that there were circumstances where coaches' (and other adults') focus on the demands of the sport and the team took precedence over the rights of child athletes. Moreover, the right to appropriate guidance contains the important principle that this guidance should be in line with 'the evolving capacities of the child' to exercise them. The evidence from our own research and the wider literature suggests that coaches role in harm to children rises as children advanced through the competitive ranks, suggesting an increasingly negligent attitude to children's rights.

Utting *et al.* (1997), in their report on institutional abuse in Wales, distinguished between 'career abusers' and adults who 'are not habitual abusers but who resort to abusive conduct under stress or in corrupting environmental circumstances'. It is a distinction that may be useful in the context of coaches, with sport. In particular, the sport ethic — as a 'corrupting environmental circumstance' — can lead coaches to act in a way that is not in the best interests of children in their care and under their instruction.

CHAPTER 5

Peers as perpetrators of harmful treatment of children in sport

Introduction

In the previous chapters it has been noted that much of the research on harm to children in sport has focused on the role of coaches and other significant adults as perpetrators. The close and intense relationships that develop between coaches and their young charges, and the power relations inherent in them, can provide the breeding ground for controlling or abusive behaviour. In recognition of these dangers and of the evidence of the abuse of young athletes by their coaches in a variety of sports, a great deal of policy and practice effort has been directed at the development of effective child-protection policies and procedures in sporting organisations.

We highlighted in earlier chapters that research on peer perpetrators of harm in sport has been limited to date. Our research has helped to fill that gap. It has also provided data on the way young people involved in organised sport relate to one another: peers were the main perpetrators of harm in sport. Our study revealed that, while harmful behaviour between peers tended to be at the lower end of seriousness, it was widespread. It tended to be expected and accepted by young people, but it also impacted on the extent to which they enjoyed their participation in organised sport.

OVERVIEW OF PEERS AS PERPETRATORS OF HARM

Table 5.1 shows the proportion of respondents to our survey who reported each of the major types of harm explored in the survey and gave team mates or peers as perpetrators of the harmful treatment they experienced. As the table indicates, team mates and peers were major perpetrators of harm across all the major types of harm, in both respondents' main and second sports. Their role was particularly significant in the case of emotional harm and sexual harm, although, as we saw in Chapter 2, the numbers who reported any sexually harmful behaviour were small. Across all categories of harm, and in both main and second sport, young men were more likely than young women to report that their team mates or peers were perpetrators of harm.

Table 5.1: Percentage of respondents giving team mates/peers as perpetrators of various types of harm in main and second sport, by gender.

	Main sport			Second sport		
	Total	Male	Female	Total	Male	Female
Emotional harm	81%	87%	79%	79%	85%	77%
Physical harm	62%	71%	58%	67%	74%	65%
Sexual harassment	65%	77%	63%	66%	76%	64%
Sexual harm	88%	97%	81%	86%	100%	77%

As young people advanced in their sports, the proportion who gave their team mates and peers as a source of harm fell, with more young people giving coaches and others as perpetrators. However, team mates and peers remained the most frequent source of harmful behaviour at all levels of competition and across all types of harm, with the exception of physical harm, where coaches over-took peers as the most frequently given perpetrators.

The top seven sports in our survey had different profiles in terms of the extent to which young people reported that their peers were responsible for the harm they experienced. For example, while 29% of those who were physically harmed while doing dance as their main sport said their team mates or peers were perpetrators, this rose to 77% for those doing rugby. This is indicative of a pattern suggesting that young people taking part in team sports were more likely to report physical harm at the hands of their peers than young people who took part in more individual sports.

Young people who took part in mixed sports were more likely to report sexual harassment at the hands of their peers than those who participated in single-sex sports: for example, more than three-quarters of young people who reported sexual harassment in their main sport of swimming named peers as perpetrators, compared to just 53% in netball. However, participants in all-male sports also reported high levels of sexually harassing behaviour by team mates and peers.

Rugby players were at the greatest risk of harmful treatment at the hands of their peers. Young people playing rugby as their main sport were more likely than participants in the other top seven sports to report the involvement of peers in both emotional harm (91%) and physical harm (77%). Rugby players who reported sexual harassment and sexual harm also described a high level of team mate and peer involvement in those behaviours (68% and 91% respectively).

PEERS AS PERPETRATORS OF EMOTIONAL HARM

In Chapter 2, we noted that the limited research focusing on emotional harm in sport has examined it almost exclusively insofar as it is perpetrated by adults. It also noted that it was very commonly experienced by young people responding to our survey and that the major perpetrators were peers (see Table 5.1). Eighty-one per cent of respondents who reported emotional harm in their main sport said that their peers or team mates were involved. The equivalent figure for second sport was 79%.

The role of peers and team mates as perpetrators of emotionally harmful behaviour diminished as young athletes advanced through the competitive ranks, although they were still given by the majority of respondents as perpetrators at all levels. Eighty-three per cent of respondents who participated in their main sport at recreational level reported that their team mates or peers were involved in the emotional harm they experienced but this had dropped to 69% among young athletes who competed at international level.

Young men were more likely than young women to say their team mates or peers were responsible for the emotionally harmful behaviour they were subjected to (87% compared to 79%). This difference may be explained by the sports that they participated in. Rugby had the highest proportion of team mate involvement, 91% of those reporting emotional harm (main sport) compared to 73% in athletics, which had the lowest. Generally, team sports such as netball, football, hockey and rugby tended to have more team mate involvement in emotional harm.

Interviews with research participants revealed that specific components of emotional harm were more likely to be perpetrated by team mates and peers, with teasing and bullying behaviours being most likely to be discussed. Teasing by team mates tended to be accepted as normal by most young people in the interviews. It could focus on a range of issues: a boy doing dance was teased by his fellow dancers (mainly girls) for being involved in such a 'girly' activity; another was teased for his 'man boobs'; another for the 'double whammy' of 'being both round and having red hair'; a young woman described being teased for wearing the wrong trainers. Participants tended to dismiss these behaviours as 'banter', 'meant in a jokey way' and just 'kids being kids'. However, they could be hurtful and cause young athletes distress:

> But then at the same time there's like, I don't know, it used to hurt as well. And you used to be like, I don't know, you used to think about it and then just think twice of yourself. Like if they said something, then you think 'oh is that actually true'. (*Young woman: main sport rugby; second sport hockey*)

Where teasing remained at this sort of level, most participants described a process where their team mates and peers 'grew out of it' and respondents grew up and cared less. However, some also experienced these behaviours, and others, to the extent that they described it as bullying. Once again, young people appeared to expect and accept that they would be bullied and that this was part of the experience, both of being a child and of taking part in sport:

> I was worried about you asking me about the bullying because I think it just happens to everyone, you know, I wasn't particularly the bullied one, I think there was probably worse people and I'm sure I bullied some people as well. (*Young woman: main sport dance*)

Targets of bullying could change and the focus of bullying behaviour could be sport or other areas of young people's lives:

> You would generally find some nights at training like you would have ten, fifteen people having a pop at like one person, and it being like an onslaught, and it was just... that

was like the kind of bad side of it. … It could be anything like your skill base or your actual playing performance, even if like it wasn't an issue they would just pick something off it. It could also be like a bit of personal stuff like family stuff and things like that. (*Young man: main sport rugby; second sport football*)

Bullies often took care to shield the behaviour from coaches or other adults. Young people rarely reported telling anyone except parents about what was happening. There were examples of parents intervening and speaking to coaches and teachers and finding that the reaction was swift and effective, but in a number of cases young people reported that nothing changed.

PEERS AS PERPETRATORS OF PHYSICAL HARM

Persistent bullying and its debilitating effect on the children experiencing it is increasingly being recognised in the education literature. Its effects can lead to children refusing to go to school, to leaving or changing school, to work suffering, to serious mental health difficulties. There is increasing evidence of the effects of persistent, low-level bullying on the psychological well-being of children and young people that can be particularly difficult for young people to cope with and schools and teachers to deal with (Lloyd, 2004). Many young people reported experiencing a range of peer bullying and peer violence in a sporting context when they were children.

In common with the views expressed on emotional harm, some participants who had experienced physical harm at the hands of their peers clearly felt that some physical aggression was to be expected in sport, that it was part of the game and needed to be accepted by those taking part:

It's a physical game, get over it. If he didn't want to play a physical game then why is he playing hockey? (*Young man: main sport ice hockey; second sport football*)

They would scrap amongst themselves — when you're driving places and you put ten kids in a mini-bus what do you expect? In hockey there were fights but that was just part of the game. (*Young man: main sport ice hockey; second sport martial arts*)

Others described aggressive behaviour as a part of competition, but not as something that affected the participants badly. Another boy participating in hockey explained that it was 'not really too bad. Opposing teams always rammed each other. We were very competitive. We gave as good as we got. It wasn't really physical harm.'

However, there were also circumstances in which participants would use the sport to conceal aggressive or violent behaviour, sometimes out of the view of coaches:

In a game people would try and target me and in response I would kind of go at them as well because it's the only way to stop them because you stand there when someone just offloads you the ball then you are going to get smashed. (*Young man: main sport rugby; second sport football*)

Some participants described the way in which balls were thrown with the intention of hurting someone. For example, a girl participating in lacrosse reported that as the goalie she regularly had balls hit at her. She explained that in lacrosse you can get someone on the neck with the ball and no one really notices and that the goalie is easy to hit. She explained that this affected her quite badly but she thought it was normal in sport and she should not complain. She kept her bruises covered so her parents did not see them.

Sometimes the physical bullying and aggression seemed minor, but, in the context of other things that were happening in young people's lives, the impact was serious. For example, an incident that a coach may have observed as occurring once or as trivial could be happening repeatedly or could be echoed in other areas of the young person's life.

This young woman described how behaviour she experienced in sport affected her in other areas of her life:

In team practice, the same group of girls, the bullies, were often the opposition team and they would purposely hit you. It was only our group that they did it to ... I was worried if they were going to do something to me off the pitch or after school. I was worried about walking home on my own. I would always find people to walk with, or would go a different way home. (*Young woman: main sport trampolining; second sport rounders*)

In her case, she told her teachers and they dealt well with the situation. She also told her mum who contacted the school to make sure that they continued to deal with bullying behaviour.

. . . .

In another case, a young man who played rugby as a child described how pre-existing emotions and relationships at school were played out in rugby. He had been stabbed by compasses in school by the same boys who bullied him on the rugby field, one of whom had stamped on his ankle and broken it. As with most of the young people who experienced repeated bullying and aggression in sport and other settings he did not tell anyone about his experience.

. . . .

PEERS AND SEXUAL HARM

Most of the sexual harm disclosed in our research took the form of sexualised behaviour, and 'locker room' antics between peers, in male-dominated sports such as rugby and football. Again, young people seemed to expect that this would happen. In the words of one young man, who reported on his questionnaire return having had someone expose themselves to him: 'It was rugby, of course this happened.' In some cases, these behaviours were dismissed by participants as harmless fun:

> It was commonplace to be naked in changing rooms and bum grabbing was funny. Forced kissing on the cheeks was also funny. (*Young man: main sport football; second sport rugby*)

> I wouldn't consider this 'sexual harm'. I would consider it joking around with the lads. Nothing sexual was intended. (*Young man: main sport football; second sport cricket*)

Some comments recognised, however, that these behaviours could be uncomfortable for some and might not be appropriate:

> Teenage boys are stupid and running around naked exposing themselves to people was common and for a select few

members of the team was a staple. It could be uncomfortable or funny depending on the setting. (*Young man: main sport football; second sport rugby*)

Some male to female behaviour was reported in more mixed sports such as swimming. Some young people laughed this off at the time:

> Boys at the competition at swimming would find it a great joke to run into the girls changing rooms and flash their bits at us. That was quite common. but they were just little boys being little boys really ... The coaches would be like, you know, 'leave off', but it was never anything serious. They never got sent out of swimming or anything for it. It was always 'pack it in lads'. (*Young woman: main sport kayaking; second sport swimming*)

At the time, this young woman found this behaviour to be immature but not upsetting. Looking back, although she was aware it was not actively condoned by coaches, she thought it was 'gross' and that adults should have done more to prevent it from happening.

There were more serious reports. The example below highlights the way incidents can flare up out of sight of coaches and supervisory adults, the vulnerability of some young people and the long lasting effects of some of the behaviours.

A young gay man described an incident when he was forced to kiss another boy:
> It was ... like, how do I describe it. Like ... when you put on weight it looks like you have breasts as a boy. [There were] jokes about page three and things like that. Like when you are ten, eleven and twelve, kids know nothing about ... it would be like — 'oh you're turning into a girl!' And then it was like, 'boys kiss girls'. You kiss each other, like that — they wouldn't let me out of the changing rooms before I went along with what they wanted ... and obviously five minutes can seem like five hours when you are a child. You are like, no I need to go, I need to go now, I'm going to be in trouble. And so maybe another thirty seconds went on and it just got worse. So I mean it would only be like a few seconds but then,

> I'd, you know, and I could say that was more of a big deal than sort of like the fat jokes.

This boy left sport altogether without explaining to anyone why he was doing so:

> So, I'd you know, I probably in the car on the way home would have probably have said that, well not said what happened but said that 'oh I'm just getting a bit bored with all this now' and dress it up as me not wanting to do it any more. (*Young man: main sport swimming*)

ADULTS' AWARENESS OF HARMFUL BEHAVIOUR FROM PEERS

In the previous chapter, the issue of adults' awareness of potentially harmful behaviour and failure to deal with it adequately was raised with specific reference to sexual harassment. Throughout our research, it was also raised in relation to other forms of behaviour, particularly from peers. Some young people when they reflected on their experiences of bullying thought that the adults involved knew what was going on even if they had not been told:

> Yeah, the coaches, they were never too naïve to think that this wasn't going to happen, because a lot of these guys have played themselves, and they didn't just get their coaching qualification because their kid was in the team. They did it because they liked playing themselves, and their son just like picked up from them. So yeah, I think they knew from their own experience that it was going to happen. (*Young man: main sport ice hockey; second sport football*)

One young man speculated about why adults did not intervene in bullying behaviour which they either knew or should have known was going on. He wondered whether they just did not want to deal with it or were insufficiently qualified to deal with it. Some young people described this failure to deal with bullying as negligent but, perhaps surprisingly, others looked back and thought that these situations could leave coaches in a difficult position:

> It's difficult isn't it because I mean … you don't, it's that fine line. You don't want to have to place the teacher in

the changing rooms and leave them open to questions. And you, if you are not telling the teachers what's going on they've got no way of knowing what's going on. (*Young man: main sport swimming*)

One young man described how he thought it should be dealt with:

Probably not to do anything about it until either, one, it became offensive, really offensive to the adult or, two, it became really offensive to the child, it was affecting the child in the sense that they didn't want to play the sport any more. It affected their performance or it was causing obvious … it affected them physically or anything like that. I'm, to a certain extent, I've a sort of hard-nosed approach. It's an experience most people tend to go through. And you tend to go through it yourself. And it makes you, to a certain extent, stronger and you know what's going to happen. You know how to approach it in future. (*Young man: main sport rugby, second sport bowls*)

Such an approach relies on coaches' judgements about the level of bullying behaviour that was acceptable, rather than considering the views of the child athletes concerned. But it echoed the experience of a number of young people who were told, by both parents and coaches, that they needed to 'toughen up' or that what they were experiencing was 'character building' — further evidence of the strength of the sport ethic, even at lower levels of sport. Some young people found this effective:

You just sort of get into a mentality, not that you're better than them, but that you're … they're sort of jocks: sporty, thick-headed people, and you know, you may not be as great as them but at least you're giving it a shot and at least you don't do that to other people, and at least you are above that sort of thing. (*Young man: main sport badminton; second sport athletics*)

But for others, this approach was hard to understand and made organised sport the location of experiences that in other areas of

their lives, where their interests and views were taken into consideration more routinely, would be unacceptable:

> Yeah, there was something that wasn't right, because that
> was the only place that I ever got treated like that. You know,
> it wasn't like that at school, the kids were fine to me, it wasn't
> like that at home, this was the only place. But again it was
> just kind of drilled into you from anywhere and everywhere,
> if you wanted to be good, if you wanted to keep going, then
> this is what you have to do, this is what you have to put up
> with, and everyone put up with it. (*Young woman: main
> sport gymnastics*)

CONCLUSION

This chapter has considered the role of peers as the perpetrators of harm to other
young people in sport, focusing on the areas of emotional, physical and sexual
harm, areas that we noted in the last chapter are explicitly dealt with by UNCRC.
Peers are the major perpetrators of harm in all these areas, but, as their testimony shows, the young people involved in the research often were reluctant to
view these behaviours as harmful and tended to see them as just what happens
in sport and to be both expected and accepted.

The research explicitly considered the experience of children and young
people in organised sport settings, that is, those where they are under the
care and instruction of adults. The chapter has therefore also touched on the
awareness of adults of these behaviours and their role in challenging it and in
developing a respectful sporting culture in which the interests of the child are
paramount. Young people expressed a certain confusion on these matters, born
of their belief that they must learn to accept the behaviours this chapter has
considered if they wish to continue with their sporting endeavours. They did
not like what was happening to them and thought adults knew or should know,
but often thought there was nothing that the adults could do to eliminate it.
The next chapter examines further young people's views on how sport can be a
more positive experience for them, and it also discusses recent developments
to support that vision.

CHAPTER 6

Summary and conclusion

INTRODUCTION

This book has set out information from a three-year study examining the experiences, including harmful experiences, of children participating in organised sport in the UK. The study combined a literature review with information from an online survey (yielding more than 6,000 returns) from young people (aged eighteen to twenty-two) who had been asked to reflect on their experiences of participating in organised sport as children; and also from eighty-nine detailed follow-up interviews.

Prior research addressing the issue of harm to children in sport has tended to focus on: the experiences of young élite athletes; on certain kinds of abuse, mainly sexual abuse and harassment; and on certain kinds of sports such as gymnastics and swimming. Previous chapters in the book have provided new insights into the experiences of boys and girls participating in sport at all levels and from more than forty different sports.

In analysing our data, we viewed young people's reported experiences of sport through the prism of children's rights and the minimum standards for their care and protection as set out in the UN Convention on the Rights of the Child (UNCRC). The Convention addresses, among other things, children's right to health, protection against maltreatment, abuse and exploitation, to freedom of expression and to have their views taken into account. All of these have direct relevance for the welfare and rights of children participating in sport.

In general, sport research literature tends to present sport as a universal positive in young people's lives. Indeed, in our study, too, young people reported that the positives of sport outweighed the negatives. It was fun, enjoyable, friendly, co-operative and exciting. They enjoyed the social aspects of sport, learning skills, keeping fit and healthy, being active and part of a team. Sport could build confidence and provide a sense of achievement. However, sitting alongside these positive things about sport, young people also reported negative experiences and we have explored these around the separate categories of sexual harm, physical harm and emotional harm.

SPORTING CULTURES

Our study has highlighted that low-level, disrespectful and negative treatment of children in sport is widespread. In previous chapters we attempted to explain this with reference to other sport research that discusses the 'sport ethic', where athletes are inculcated into a culture in sport where ignoring injuries and playing through pain are accepted as normal. Young people in our study provided accounts of how, early in their sporting lives, they were inculcated into the 'sport ethic'. They learned that success and affirmation in sport are gained through accepting pain and discomfort, and by putting up with and accepting as normal, disrespectful, negative, hurtful and emotionally harmful treatment. From an early age these young people learned to accept and deal with issues on their own and without complaint, also to put up with pain. In team sports they often trained though injury 'for the good of the team'. In individual sports, particularly those such as gymnastics and dance, where there could be an intensive relationship between athlete and coach, and where coaches expected and received a high level of commitment, young people described gruelling regimes where it seemed like the imperative of competition took precedence over young people's well-being and welfare. Some described putting their bodies 'beyond physical limitations' and training through tears.

Children and Organised Sport has also shed light on who was involved in perpetrating harmful and disrespectful treatment of children in sport and of the circumstances in which it occurred. While our study has suggested that much of the treatment described by young people was the result of activity between young people themselves, the involvement of coaches and other sporting adults was also fairly widespread, either directly or in accepting and condoning the ill treatment or not effectively dealing with it.

THE ROLE OF COACHES AND OTHER ADULTS IN HARM TO CHILDREN

The UNCRC is helpful in clarifying minimum standards of care for protecting and promoting the rights of children in any setting. However, for many of the young people in our study, it was clear that sporting adults were not providing care and protection at levels that met the standards set out in the UN Convention. Adults were directly involved in sexual, physical and emotional harm of children. There were instances where coaches' demands took precedence over children's emotional and physical needs and welfare.

Coaches played a key role in instilling a culture where children came to accept pain and injury as an integral part of participating in sport. They encouraged young people to train excessively or through injury and exhaustion. While some of this seemed relatively benign, there were instances where young people were forced to train on when ill or injured in ways that seemed dangerous. In some cases, young people experienced it as distressing but found it difficult to speak up to coaches, either because they were afraid of them, in awe of them or did not want to appear weak.

There were a few instances where physical aggression and violence were used by coaches as a means of control and punishment; sometimes it was the result of frustration and anger at young people's performance which spilled over, leading to coaches lashing out at young athletes. In these small number of cases, not only were coaches not meeting minimum standards of care set out in the UN Convention but they were also breaking UK law.

There were many instances of negative emotionally harmful treatment of young athletes by coaches being used as a coaching tool. Young people reported being shouted at, sworn at and being subjected to humiliating and belittling treatment. Coaches used negative behaviour and emotionally harmful behaviour to extract better performance from young people. This was experienced at both élite and recreational levels of sport.

A key finding from the research was the extent to which young people were exposed to sexually harassing behaviour. Much of this occurred between young people; but coaches were also involved, either directly perpetrating it, in condoning it or not effectively dealing with it. Direct involvement by coaches mainly concerned comments about young people's clothes, weight and appearance. This was exacerbated in the context of young people reaching puberty, feeling embarrassed about their changing bodies and how they looked in the context of having to wear revealing sport gear. Some young people experienced this as distressing. Sexist comments and comments about appearance by passers-by in team sports played outside could also cause embarrassment.

THE ROLE OF OTHER CHILDREN

Our study sheds new light on the way young people treat each other in the context of sport. Most of the harm that occurred to children in our study was harm they did to each other.

Eighty-one percent of young people who reported emotional harm in sport said their peers or team mates were involved. It was more common at recreational and lower levels of sport than at élite level and more common in team sports such as rugby, football, netball and hockey. Teasing and bullying were most common. Most young people dismissed this as banter and 'not serious'. For others, it could be distressing and have lasting implications. Notably, young people rarely reported what was happening.

Physical harm was also relatively widespread among peers. Again, much of this was at the less serious end and accepted as normal. There were other instances where participants used sport to conceal aggressive and violent behaviour from coaches. Most young people endured this without complaint either because they accepted it as just what happens in sport or because they were fearful of the coach or did not want to seem weak in the eyes of coaches or peers.

Most of the sexual harm disclosed took the form of 'locker room antics' between peers in mainly male sports of rugby and football. Again this was often dismissed as harmless fun but some young people described high levels of discomfort and found it distressing. This could be worse where young people were particularly vulnerable, as in the case of homophobic bullying.

ENSURING CHILDREN ARE SAFE AND HAPPY IN SPORT

Young people involved in the research for this book were asked to reflect back on their experiences of sport as children. Since then a range of policy developments and legislative change designed to keep children safe in a range of settings, including sport, have been introduced.

At the legislative level, since the turn of the century there has been considerable and rapid developments in 'Vetting and Barring' – the systems designed to prevent unsuitable adults from working with children. Separate systems for vetting and barring are in place across the UK, with differences in their scope and operation. But they share in common the aim of assisting in preventing unsuitable people from working with children. Government advice is clear, however, that while vetting and barring can prevent people known to be unsuitable from working with children, they cannot ensure that a person is suitable to work with children. The systems should be used as part of an organisation's overall child protection policy (Smith, 2010). In the case of sports organisations, the last decade has seen a great deal of activity on the part of national, regional and local organisations to keep children safe and happy while participating in sport.

Established in 2001, the Child Protection in Sport Unit (CPSU) is a partnership between the NSPCC, Sport England, Sports Council Northern Ireland and the Sports Council for Wales. Its counterpart in Scotland, Safeguarding in Sport, is a partnership between Children 1st and sportscotland. Both the CPSU and Safeguarding in Sport work with governing bodies and other organisations to minimise risk to children in sport. Their work includes developing practical resources for sports organisations; developing training programmes for child welfare in sport; and providing advice to sports organisations and others.

An important output of these partnerships has been the development of national standards or frameworks for each of the home nations, setting out good practice in safeguarding and protecting children in sport. Set within the context of the generic safeguarding and child protection policy established since 2000 by the UK government and by each of the devolved parliaments or assemblies in Northern Ireland, Wales and Scotland, each of the nations has developed different standards or frameworks (Sport England, 2003a; Sports Council Wales, 2006; Child Protection in Sport Steering Group, 2006; Volunteer Development Agency, 2009; Sport Northern Ireland, 2010).

The specific elements within the standards or frameworks vary across the constituent parts of the UK. The home nations also vary in the extent to which achievement of certain standards is a prerequisite for funding for sports organisations. However, they all have aspects in common. Each expects that sports organisations have policies and procedures in place to protect and safeguard children, that these policies and procedures go beyond minimum legal requirements and that they should be monitored and evaluated.

Changes at the legislative and policy level described above are relevant to individual children at club level. The national standards and frameworks have established clear expectations on all sports clubs for children on how they should operate. The CPSU (and its counterpart in Scotland) supports sports clubs to develop in line with the standards and provides resources to assist clubs in drawing up their policies and practices. These include sample policies; codes of practice for coaches, parents and spectators; and anti-bullying resources. In addition, individual sports' governing bodies have produced guidance for their sports.

These developments have been explicitly informed by a children's rights agenda. In all parts of the UK, the standards or frameworks make specific reference to rights. For example, in England, Standards for Safeguarding and Protecting Children in Sport begins by setting out the principles underpinning the standards:

- Children and young people have a right to enjoy sport, free from all forms of abuse and exploitation
- All children and young people have equal rights to protection from harm
- All children and young people should be encouraged to fulfil their potential and inequalities should be challenged
- Everybody has a responsibility to support the care and protection of children
- Sporting organisations have a duty of care to the children and young people who take part in sport (Sport England, 2003a, p. 4)

These principles reflect rights enshrined in the UNCRC, specifically, the principle of best interests of the child (Article 3), the right to protection form maltreatment, exploitation and abuse (Article 19 and 33), the right to leisure and play (Article 31) and the right to equality and non-discrimination (Article 2). They are expected to inform the safeguarding and child protection policies and procedures that sports organisations have in place and guide their implementation.

The extent to which these measures together have made a demonstrable difference to young people's experiences of organised sport in the UK and have addressed some of the issues raised by young people in this study remains to be seen. It would be interesting to repeat this research in five or ten years' time using the information in this study as a baseline to gauge the extent to which new polices designed to protect children have been effective in making a positive difference to the lives, safety and enjoyment of children participating in sport. Repetition of the study would also allow a judgement to be made about the extent to which the issues young people themselves thought were important had become part of the landscape of organised sport for children.

WHAT YOUNG PEOPLE WANT

We asked young people for their views on measures that should be put in place to keep children safe and happy in sport. Many were aware that legislative, policy and practice developments had been made in this area since they were children. They mentioned requirements to vet people who worked with children and were generally supportive of these measures. Young people also wanted to ensure that vetting information remained up to date and that checks on people were repeated periodically. Some young people who had remained involved in sport as volunteers or coaches were also aware that many changes had taken place at club level to ensure children's welfare. They spoke of clubs' child protection policies and procedures. They also spoke of changes in coaching practice including the move to a more 'holistic' coaching practice, based on the notion that 'a happy person makes a happy athlete'.

However, young participants also thought that keeping children safe and happy in sport was about more than legal and formal structures. Many of the suggestions made during the research focused on the atmosphere and ethos of clubs. Below we set out what young people in the study told us about new mechanisms they wanted to see put in place to ensure sport for children was safe and fun.

Addressing bullying and emotional harm

Young people were concerned that adults involved should be aware of the way in which young people interact with one another and should be aware of behaviours that could be upsetting to young people or that could escalate to bullying. Young people were sometimes concerned that bullying would always be a part of children's lives, and that adults could never know what went on behind their backs, but this concern should not impede efforts to prevent it, or to promote a culture in which it was unacceptable. This concern for respectful treatment of children extended to the behaviour of adults, whether they were coaches, trainers, parents or other adults involved with sport for children.

Addressing exclusion

There was also a concern that sport for children should be inclusive and open to all. The question of inclusiveness had a number of elements for research participants. One was the question of sporting ability. Concerns were raised that, in many clubs, a hierarchy developed according to sporting ability and this led to the exclusion of less talented players. Many research participants thought this was inappropriate in children's sport and that access to instruction and adult attention should not be dependent on ability. The promotion of an inclusive social environment within sport was also important, and this was linked to bullying. Participants referred to the formation of 'cliques' and 'in crowds' that affected the enjoyment of children who did not fit into such groupings. Some participants also spoke of financial exclusion and the concern that some children missed out on opportunities because sport for children was inadequately funded.

Addressing the imperative of winning over welfare

Young people also wanted to make sure that the fun elements of sport were not sacrificed to the demands of competition and the pursuit of excellence. Participants were aware that, while competition was an important element of sport at all levels, for most children sport would remain recreational and getting the balance wrong and placing too great an emphasis on competition could destroy the enjoyment of sport.

Our study raises serious questions about the role coaches and other adults play in effectively challenging and dealing with negative and harmful behaviour in sport. It is clear from the research that young people would value a sporting ethos that supports coaching based on positive encouragement, open communication and more participative practices. This would build towards the kind of sporting experience young people told us they would value, that is, one that is social, inclusive and enables children to progress positively in their sport in ways that allow them to feel good about themselves at whatever level they participate. Much of this was articulately summed up by one young woman who took part in the study:

> It should definitely be made sure that the trainers are good, mature, responsible and know what an impact they are making on the children — they should definitely be trained to understand complex issues such as fairness and bullying, and how bad experiences have an impact on the whole lives of children. No bullying should be allowed at all, everyone should be allowed to participate, and no negative comments should be made about any of the children by any adults, as that can have a devastating effect. This should also be made clear to all parents. It would also be extremely helpful if there were many more recreational sports clubs, as I feel that those would be most helpful to the majority of children, who just want to have fun with sports. This would also have a very positive impact on how they see and participate in sport also in the future. (*Young woman: main sport martial arts; second sport rounders*)

References

American Academy of Pediatrics (2000) 'Intensive training and sports specialisation in young athletes', *Pediatrics*, Vol. 106, No. 1, Pt 1, pp. 154–7

Brackenridge, C. (2001) *Spoilsports: Understanding and Preventing Sexual Exploitation in Sport*, London: Routledge

Brackenridge, C. (2002) '"… so what?" Attitudes of the voluntary sector towards child protection in sports clubs', *Managing Leisure*, pp. 7103–23

Brackenridge, C. (2008) 'Violence and abuse prevention in sport', in Kaufman, K. (ed.), London: Brunel University, School of Sport and Education Research Papers; http://bura.brunel.ac.uk/handle/2438/2789 (accessed March 2011)

Brackenridge, C., Bringer, J. and Bishopp, D. (2005) 'Managing cases of abuse in sport', *Child Abuse Review*, Vol. 14, No. 4, pp. 259–74

Brackenridge, C. and Kirby, S. (1997) 'Playing safe? Assessing the risk of sexual abuse to young elite athletes', *International Review for the Sociology of Sport*, Vol. 32, No. 4, pp. 407–18

Brackenridge, C., Rivers, I., Gough, B. and Llewellyn, K. (2006) 'Driving down participation: Homophobic bullying as a deterrent to doing sport', in Aitchison, C. (ed.) (2006) *Sport and Gender Identities: Masculinities, Femininities and Sexualities*, London: Routledge

Brenner, J. S. (2007) 'Overuse injuries, overtraining, and burnout in child and adolescent athletes', *Pediatrics*, Vol. 119, No. 6, pp. 1242–5

Bringer, J. D., Brackenridge, C. H. and Johnston, L. H. (2006) 'Swimming coaches' perceptions of sexual exploitation in sport: A preliminary model of role conflict and role ambiguity', *The Sport Psychologist*, Vol. 20, pp. 465–79

Cawson, P., Wattam, C., Brooker, S. and Kelly, G. (2000) *Child Maltreatment in the United Kingdom – A Study of the Prevalence of Child Abuse and Neglect*, London: NSPCC

Cense, M. and Brackenridge, C. (2001) 'Temporal and developmental risk factors for sexual harrassment and abuse in sport', *European Physical Education Review*, Vol. 7, No. 1, pp. 61–79

Child Protection in Sport Steering Group (2006) *2006 Accord for the Protection of Children in Scottish Sport*, Glasgow: Child Protection in Sport Service

Coakley, J. (1992) 'Burnout among adolescent athletes: A personal failure or social problem?', *Sociology of Sport Journal*, pp. 9271–85

Coakley, J. (2007) *Sport in Society: Issues and Controversies*, London: McGraw Hill

Coleman, L., Cox, L. and Roker, D. (2008) 'Girls and young women's participation in physical activity: Psychological and social influences', *Health Education Research*, Vol. 23, No. 4, pp. 633–47

Creighton, S. (2002) *Physical Abuse*, London: NSPCC

David, P. (2005) *Human Rights in Youth Sport: A Critical Review of Children's Rights in Competitive Sports*, London: Routledge

Dong, M., Anda, R. F., Dube, S. R., Giles, W. H. and Felitti, V. J. (2003) 'The relationship of exposure to childhood sexual abuse to other forms of abuse, neglect, and household dysfunction during childhood', *Child Abuse & Neglect*, Vol. 27, No. 6, pp. 625–39

Evans, H. (2002) *Emotional Abuse*, London: NSPCC

Farstad, S. (2007) 'Protecting children's rights in sport: The use of minimum age', *Human Rights Law Commentary*, Nottingham: University of Nottingham; http://www.nottingham.ac.uk/hrlc/publications/humanrightslawcommentary.aspx (accessed March 2011)

Fasting, K. (2005) 'Research on sexual harassment and abuse in sport', *idrottsforum* [*Nordic Sport Science Web Journal*]; http://www.idrottsforum.org/articles/fasting/fasting050405.html (accessed March 2011)

Fasting, K., Brackenridge, C. and Sundgot-Borgen, J. (2004) 'Prevalence of sexual harassment among Norwegian female elite athletes in relation to sport type', *International Review for the Sociology of Sport*, Vol. 39, No. 4, pp. 373–86

Finch, N. (2001) *Young People with a Disability and Sport*, London: Sport England

Foster, C., Hillsdon, M., Cavill, N., Allender, S. and Cowburn, G. (2005) *Understanding Participation in Sport: A Systematic Review*, London: Sport England

Gallagher, B. (2000) 'The extent and nature of known cases of institutional child sexual abuse', *British Journal of Social Work*, Vol. 30, No. 6, pp. 795–817

Gervis, M. and Dunn, N. (2004) 'The emotional abuse of elite child athletes by their coaches', *Child Abuse Review*, Vol. 13, pp. 215–23

Hartill, M. (2009) 'The sexual abuse of boys in organised male sports', *Men and Masculinities*, Vol. 12, No. 2, pp. 225–49

Hughes, M. (ed.) (2009) *Social Trends*, Newport: Office for National Statistics; http://www.statistics.gov.uk/downloads/theme_social/Social_Trends39/Social_Trends_39.pdf (accessed March 2011)

Killick, L. (2009) *'Walking the Fine Line?': Young People, Sporting Risk, Health and Embodied Identities*, Loughborough: Loughborough University

Kirby, S., Greaves, L. and Hankinsky, O. (2000) *The Dome of Silence: Sexual Harassment and Abuse in Sport*, London: Zed Books

Leahy , T., Pretty, G. and Tenenbaum, G. (2002) 'Prevalence of sexual abuse in organised competitive sport in Australia', *Journal of Sexual Aggression*, Vol. 8, No. 2, pp. 16–36

Lloyd, G. (ed.) (2004) *Problem Girls: Working with the Troubled and Troublesome*, London: Routledge

Maffulli, N. and Pintore, E. (1990) 'Intensive training in young athletes', *British Journal of Sports Medicine*, Vol. 24, No. 4, pp. 237–9

Malcolm, N. (2006) ' "Shaking it off" and "toughing it out": Socialisation to pain and injury in girls' softball', *Journal of Contemporary Ethnography*, Vol. 35, No. 5, pp. 495–525

Myers, J. and Barret, B. (2002) *In at the Deep End: A New Insight for all Sports from Analysis of Child Abuse within Swimming*, London: NSPCC

Nielsen, J. T. (2001) 'The forbidden zone: Intimacy, sexual relations and misconduct in the relationship between coaches and athletes', *International Review for the Sociology of Sport*, Vol. 36, No. 2, pp. 165–82

Niven, A., Fawkner, S., Knowles, A. and Henretty, J. (2009) 'From primary to secondary school: Changes in Scottish girls' physical activity and the influence of maturation and perceptions of competence', in Research Report No. 113, Edinburgh: sportscotland

Smith, A., Thurston, M., Green, K. and Lamb, K. (2007) 'Young people's participation in extracurricular physical education: A study of 15–16 year olds in North-West England and North-East Wales', *European Physical Education Review*, Vol. 13, No. 3, pp. 339–68

Smith, C. (2009) *Working with Children: Vetting and Barring – Legislation and Policy in Scotland*, Edinburgh: The University of Edinburgh/NSPCC Centre for UK-wide Learning in Child Protection

Smith, C. (2010) *Working with Children: Vetting and Barring – Legislation and Policy in England and Wales*, Edinburgh: The University of Edinburgh/ NSPCC Centre for UK-wide Learning in Child Protection

Sport England (2003a) *Standards for Safeguarding and Protecting Children in Sport*, London: Sport England

Sport England (2003b) *Young People and Sport: National Survey 2002*, London: Sport England

Sport Northern Ireland (2010) *Club Framework for Safeguarding Standards in Sport*, Belfast: NSPCC

sportscotland (2008) *Sports Participation in Scotland 2007*, Edinburgh: sportscotland

Sports Council Wales (2006) *A Framework for Safeguarding and Protecting Children in and through Sport in Wales*, Cardiff: Sports Council Wales and NSPCC; http://www.nspcc.org.uk/Inform/cpsu/resources/publications/ FrameworkForSafeguardingEnglish_wdf65596.pdf (accessed March 2011)

Sports Council Wales (2009) *Young People's Participation in Sport*, Cardiff: Sports Council Wales, Sports Update; http://www.sportwales.org.uk/ media/346127/update_65(62)_e.pdf (accessed March 2011)

Stirling, A. E. (2009) 'Definition and constituents of maltreatment in sport: Establishing a conceptual framework for research practitioners', *British Journal of Sports Medicine*, Vol. 43, No. 14, pp. 1091–9

Stirling, A. E. and Kerr, G. A. (2007) 'Elite female swimmers' experiences of emotional abuse across time', *Journal of Emotional Abuse*, Vol. 7, No. 4, pp. 89–113

Stirling, A. E. and Kerr, G. A. (2008) 'Defining and categorising emotional abuse in sport', *European Journal of Sport Science*, Vol. 8, No. 4, pp. 173–81

United Nations (1989) *Convention on the Rights of the Child*, UN General Assembly resolution 44/25 on 20 November 1989, New York: UN

Utting, W., Baines, C. and Stuart, M. (1997) *People Like Us: The Report of the Review of the Safeguards for Children Living Away from Home*, London: Stationery Office

Vanden Auweele, Y., Opdenacker, J., Vertommen, T., Boen, F., Van Niekerk, L., De Martelaer, K. and De Cuyper, B. (2008) 'Unwanted sexual experiences in sport: Perceptions and reported prevalence among Flemish female student-athletes', *International Journal of Sport & Exercise Psychology*, Vol. 6, No. 4, pp. 354–65

Volkwein, K. A. E., Schnell, F. I., Sherwood, D. and Livezey, A. (1997) 'Sexual harassment in sport: Perceptions and experiences of American female student-athletes', *International Review for the Sociology of Sport*, Vol. 32, pp. 283–95

Volunteer Development Agency (2009) *Getting It Right: Standards of Good Practice for Child Protection*, Belfast: VDA

Whitfield, C. L., Dube, S. R., Felitti, V. J. and Anda, R. F. (2005) 'Adverse childhood experiences and hallucinations', *Child Abuse & Neglect*, Vol. 29, pp. 797–810